A Sampler of
NORWAY'S FOLK COSTUMES

A Sampler of
NORWAY'S FOLK COSTUMES

BY

Thorbjørg Hjelmen Ugland

Translated by Ann Clay Zwick and Brit Henschien

BOKSENTERET FORLAG

Contents

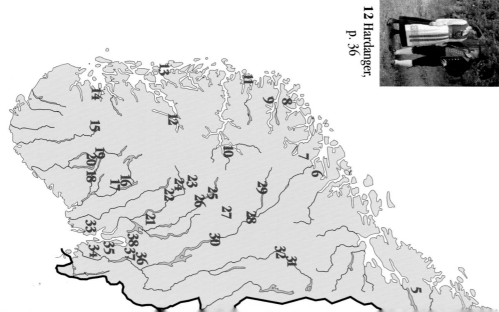

4

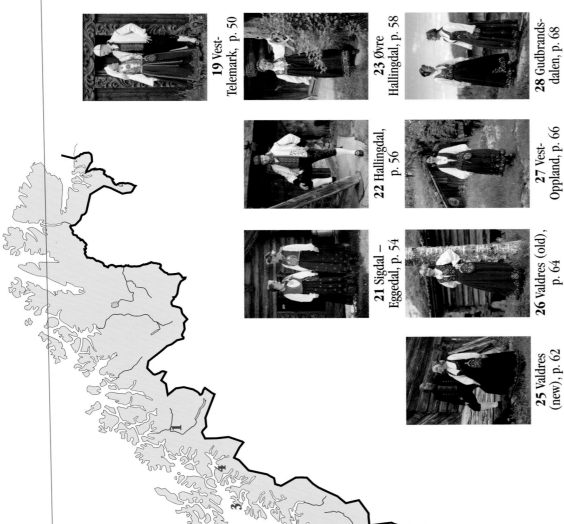

20 Vest-Telemark, p. 52

24 Nedre Hallingdal, p. 60

29 Graffer and Rondastakk, p. 70

35 Follo, p. 82

19 Vest-Telemark, p. 50

23 Øvre Hallingdal, p. 58

28 Gudbrands-dalen, p. 68

34 Østfold, p. 80

22 Hallingdal, p. 56

27 Vest-Oppland, p. 66

33 Vestfold, p. 78

Care and storage, p. 90

21 Sigdal – Eggedal, p. 54

26 Valdres (old), p. 64

32 Marie Aaen, p. 76

38 Oslo p. 88

25 Valdres (new), p. 62

31 Nord-Østerdal, p. 74

37 Romerike (L46 and man's costume), p. 86

30 Lundeby, p. 72

36 Romerike (L40, L55), p. 84

This exhibition of folk costumes and head-dresses was created for a meeting of the Rural Youth Association in Oslo in 1961. Photo: Heimen Husflid

Foreword

Hulda Garborg in her "Hulda Garborg costume," a simplified Hallingdal costume which was once worn throughout Norway. It is now exhibited at The Norwegian Theatre in Oslo. The picture is from a postcard.

We are living in an age when the world is becoming smaller. Each day, we are confronted with important events occurring on the other side of the globe. In a world filled with so many impressions, we need to establish a foothold of our own, a feeling of being securely anchored in our own culture and history. I believe this need has contributed to our recently renewed interest in wearing our national costumes. These traditional garments represent a special feeling of security and sense of belonging, to ourselves and to others.

This book is not meant to be an encyclopedia of Norwegian folk costumes. I have wanted to share my knowledge about a handful of Norwegian costumes. Some of them have never appeared in a book before, while others have. I have tried to present a selection from most regions in Norway. Of course many more should have been included, and some might have preferred a different selection. Nevertheless, these are the ones that I have chosen.

I have worked with national costumes for more than thirty years, and over the years, my respect has grown in terms of the accomplishments of others – all over Norway. Women and men have invested a great deal of time and effort and because of this, we have a wealth of national costumes. The fact that these enthusiastic souls have existed, and still exist today, fills me with gratitude.

I hope this book will be a source of pleasure and inspiration.

Thorbjørg Hjelmen Ugland
Oslo, January 18, 1996

A group from Bykle in Setesdal in about 1890, wearing folk costumes. The boy has the same costume as the men. Borrowed from the Norwegian Folk Museum. Photo: Axel Lindahl

Historical summary

Folk costumes, and how they are worn and made today, are not an old tradition but one that has developed in this century.

Toward the end of the last century, folk costumes were hardly used at all. Mass-produced clothing and fabric had gained its foothold, and in all of Norway, people dressed in the fashions of the times – influenced by the fashion of Europe. Folk costumes were only worn in a few strongholds, such as Setesdal, Hallingdal, Telemark, and a few areas of western Norway.

National romanticism was on the rise in the late 1800s. Norway was searching for its national identity, and those who lived in cities, or had moved to the cities, looked upon the culture and traditions of rural Norway with nostalgia. Interest in folk costumes increased, and by about 1890, the Hardanger costume, later known as the "national" costume, was worn throughout Norway. It was even worn in areas that had also kept their own folk costume traditions.

At this time, Hulda Garborg, a pioneer in the preservation of cultural tradition, was lecturing and giving lessons to folk dancing groups in all of Norway. She noticed the prevalence of the Hardanger costume, and encouraged people to revive their own folk costume traditions. She published Norway's first book on folk costumes, "Norsk klædebunad" (Norwegian Attire) in 1903.

Hulda Garborg wanted to preserve the genuine Norwegian elements in these costumes, but she also wanted to adapt them for modern use. In her search for suitable costumes from different regions in Norway, she followed a personal set of guidelines. The fabric was to

Above: A jacket from Telemark. Below: A woman from Sigdal. Borrowed from the Norwegian Folk Museum.

Antique silk vests and a pair of leather knee-britches. Borrowed from the Norwegian Folk Museum.

be Norwegian, and woolen embroidery was a must. If it was not possible to find complete costumes, accessories such as hats, aprons and purses, could be used as models. This method of "composing" a folk costume is still in force today. Some may think she over-simplified a complicated process, but her ideas should be judged from the perspective of her time, and what she knew about folk costumes. Hulda Garborg certainly prepared the groundwork for our present unique folk costume tradition, which is a source of pride to all of us.

Klara Semb was a member of one of Hulda Garborg's folk dancing groups. She eventually succeeded her as leader, and she too taught folk dancing throughout Norway. This enabled her to learn a great deal about folk costumes also. Klara Semb had strict requirements for quality. As she said in an interview on her eightieth birthday, her mission was to stop the use of the changed and modernized costumes, and return to faithful copies in terms of color, line, embroidery, and silver ornaments. She chose to continue the use of imported materials for those costumes that used them in the past.

In 1947, Klara Semb helped found the National Council for Folk Costumes. The council's name has changed a few times, but its function is the same; it is an advisory council which has its main office in Fagernes. Contrary to what many think, it is not a council that gives a seal of approval to folk costumes. No one has this authority in Norway.

The Norwegian Council for Folk Costumes gives guidance in registering and reconstructing historic folk costumes. It assists in fabric selection, and maintains an archive of fabric, ribbon, and woolen yarns and other materials.

The Norwegian Council for Folk Costumes published a pamphlet in 1980 and defined folk costumes in the following way:

An old hat from Ulefoss, decorated with lace and beads. Borrowed from the Norwegian Folk Museum.

I Costumes representing the continuous preservation of a tradition. Folk costumes for festive occasions which were still in use when interest in wearing them enjoyed a revival.

II Costumes based on traditions which had fallen into disuse, but had not been forgotten. Many had kept these old costumes and had a general idea of what they looked like; some even began to wear them.

III Costumes that have been systematically reconstructed on the basis of preserved historic folk costume garments from the same region, era, and category. Use is made of all other documentation describing style; for example, written, pictorial and oral sources.

IV Costumes based on assumptions and incomplete historical material. Costume pieces that were not documented and are developed on the basis of existing pieces.

V Costumes that are freely composed, wholly or partially, or having patterns from articles other than clothing.

Our costumes are a unique national treasure. More than ever before, we are wearing our costumes for festive occasions. Buying a festive costume is a lifetime investment. Wearing one bears witness to our ancestral roots. A few years ago, costumes were chosen on the basis of their appearance rather than their origin. This trend has changed. Today, Norwegians establish their identity by wearing the costume that comes from the home of their forefathers.

This special belt, decorated with pressed metal plates, is attached to a band of leather or fabric. Borrowed from the Norwegian Folk Museum.

Queen Maud in 1905, wearing a Hardanger costume and its distinctive head-dress for married women. She is wearing more dress-silver than was usual at that time. Borrowed from the Norwegian Folk Museum.

Queen Sonja ordered a folk costume before she married in 1968. Since her ancestors came from Aust-Telemark, she chose the colorful costume from this region.

Ingeborg Stenseth was responsible for the embroidery, but when it was completed, she was not satisfied. The work would have to be done again. Time was of the essence, and she found a unique and radical solution. Different sections were sent to Norway's most skilled seamstresses. The fact that women from different regions in Norway were embroidering a folk costume for their future Queen had a special symbolism.

Andrea Kjærvik assembled the costume. She had been somewhat skeptical about Crown Prince Harald's decision to marry a Norwegian commoner, but after accepting the job of assembling the costume, and meeting our future Queen, Andrea Kjærvik's opinion changed. She considered it a great honor to have been chosen for this job, and later commented that Sonja's waistline was almost as small as Queen Maud's had been.

Princess Märtha Louise's Aust-Telemark costume once belonged to crown Princess Märtha, who had received it as a wedding present from the Heddal Women's Association. Anne Bamle was com-

Queen Sonja and Princess Märtha Louise wearing their folk costumes from Aust-Telemark. Photo: Frits Solvang

missioned to do the embroidery, green on the skirt and apron, and red on the bodice and jacket. The costume, with its broad and beautiful embroidery, was given to the Crown Princess three months after her wedding in 1929. It was destroyed in the fire in 1930 at Skaugum, and the Crown Princess ordered a new costume from Anne Bamle, who made her an identical one.

After the wartime occupation of Norway, the costume was lost. In 1950, Crown Princess Märtha was given a new one by the Telemark district of the Norwegian Housewives' Association. Once again, Anne Bamle did the embroidery. The costume is blue, with a red jacket.

DETAILS

Fabric:
Costume: Woolen tabby or woolen broadcloth.
Blouse: Linen.

Colors: Medium blue, dark blue, or black.

Shoes: Traditional black shoes with decorative buckles.

Stockings: White or black.

Blouse: Plain neck and yoke; embroidered collar, wrist bands and front.

Jewelry: Special dress-silver has been designed for this costume; dress-silver from Gudbrandsdalen and Østerdalen can also be worn.

Outerwear: Jacket in same color as costume, or in red.

Målselv - Bardu

The Målselv valley was a remote and unpopulated area until 1787, when tax collector Jens Holmboe encouraged the impoverished farmers from Gudbrandsdalen to move to Målselv and to clear some land. More people came later, from Dovre, Setesdal and Oppdal.

The idea of designing a local costume was raised at the Målselv Home Crafts Association, but finding old garments and records was a difficult task. Although a folk costume committee was formed in 1937, little was accomplished. After a while, Guri Myre, an academic living in Oslo, joined the committee. She found a drawing of an ancient hat from Oppdal in a 1941 issue of "Norsk Ukeblad". Since many of the early immigrants to Målselv came from Oppdal, the committee decided to pattern its costume's embroidery on the design from the hat. This embroidery is also similar to the embroidery of Gudbrands-dalen. Heimen Husflid in Oslo helped design the embroidery pattern, and later it also assisted in designing the style of the costume. The original drawing of the hat, by architect Halvdan Arneberg, can be seen in *Norsk Folkekunst, Women's Work*, plate no. 30. The cut of the bodice was taken from a bodice brought to Målselv early in the 20th century. The embroidery on the blouse was composed by I. Alapnes, a teacher from Målselv. The design of the costume was completed in 1946–1947. The jacket was designed by the Målselv Home Crafts Association and Heimen in 1963–1964.

The costume consists of a bodice, skirt, hat and purse in the same color; all of these elements have some wool embroidery. Concealed hooks fasten the bodice. The skirt is softly pleated.

Nordland

WOMAN'S COSTUME

Color: Blue or green.

Fabric: Woolen broadcloth or woolen tabby.

Shawl and apron: Hand-woven in mercerized cotton, blue checked for the blue costume, green checked for the green.

Blouse: White linen with embroidery in white.

Shoes: Traditional black shoes with decorative buckles.

Stockings: White.

Jewelry: Special dress-silver has been designed for this costume.

Outerwear: Recently, a cape has been designed for this costume. It should be in wool damask, blue or green, with a yellow lining.

MAN'S COSTUME

Colors:

Garter bands: Red white and blue, with large tassels.

Silk neckerchief: Bright, multi-colored scarf

Stockings: Blue and white

Fabric: Jacket and knee-britches: Woolen broadcloth or wadmal. (Eidsnes also mentions repp, a plain-weave fabric with prominent rounded cross-wise ribs.)

Vest: Brocade or wool in red, green or blue.

Shirt: Linen.

Shoes: Traditional black shoes with buckles.

WOMAN'S COSTUME

In about 1920, the Hålogaland Youth Association started designing a woman's costume for Nordland. At that time, the Hardanger costume was popular in many parts of the country, and later, Hulda Garborg's reconstructed Hallingdal costume became equally popular. Therefore, the Folk Costume Committee determined to create a costume specifically for Nordland.

The style is copied from a silk dress which had been a common garment in Helgeland. These dresses had no embroidery, but they were decorated with silk shawls and lace. The objective was to replace the silk finery with Norwegian fabrics, and to make use of traditional woolen embroidery. The embroidery was based on designs found by Dina Kulstad on a bodice inset and a purse at a farm at Røyto. As a child, the proprietress of the farm had been given these "paintings" to hang in her playhouse.

A great deal of work was invested in designing the embroidery for this costume, and Heimen Husfliid in Oslo also worked on the project. Mrs. Anna Svare copied the embroidery on an antique silk apron from Hattfjelldal, and adapted the same pattern for a shawl. The costume's linen blouse has the same embroidery as the skirt, but in white. The Nordland costume was presented at the Hålogaland Youth Association's meeting in 1928.

The bodice and skirt are of the same color. The front and back of the bodice are embroidered. The opening on the bodice is fastened by silver clasps at the waist and the top. The skirt is softly pleated on the front and over the hips. A panel of tight shirring is on the back of the skirt.

MAN'S COSTUME

In the early 1920s, in response to increasing interest in constructing a folk costume for Nordland and Troms for men, the magazine "Midnattssol" initiated a search for remnants of antique garments. By 1923, Johs. Eidsnes felt he had enough material to start designing a costume. He was especially fortunate in finding a master tailor at Sand, near Harstad, who had sewn similar garments during his apprentice years.

Eidsnes was to be married in the following year, and the tailor agreed to sew a costume for the bridegroom. Johs. Eidsnes did not wear a hat with his costume, but he mentions that some wore tall black hats. The short black jacket has a high standing collar. There are two rows of decorative buttons on the jacket which is worn unbuttoned. The double-breasted vest has two rows of silver buttons. The knee-britches have a front flap, a row of three buttons at the knee, and a silver buckle on each knee-band. The shirt is white linen. A few years ago, a new shirt was designed with the same embroidery as the woman's blouse from Nordland.

Hamarøy

Bergljot Wicklund was responsible for researching the folk costume from Hamarøy. She found a skirt at the Nordenfjeldske Museum of Applied Art in Trondheim, but its origin was unknown. It was later learned that the skirt came from Ulvsvåg in Hamarøy, and had belonged to Maren Normann. The skirt was brown, quilted, with a delicate white border of embroidery above the red edge around the hemline.

At the same museum, Wicklund also found a blouse-like jacket from Bodø with sleeves that tapered down to the wrists, and these two garments were the basis for the final Hamarøy costume. Heimen Husflid in Oslo helped design the embroidery. An apron is optional with this costume, of-

ten made from a blue-gray brocade. The linen blouse has a shoulder gusset and is shirred at the neck with embroidery on the neck band, cuffs and chest. The embroidery was designed by Ingeborg Hemseth on the basis of a woven blanket from Hattfjelldal which was on display at the Museum of Applied Art in Oslo in 1938. The costume was completed in 1939. It has an elongated waist and is fastened with concealed hooks, four from the waist upwards, and one at the top. The skirt has a center front pleat, is pleated over the hips and shirred in the back. The apron should be 15 cm shorter than the skirt.

D E T A I L S

Colors:
Bodice: Red.
Head-dress: Red or brown.
Purse: Same color as skirt.
Skirt: Brown with a red edging.

Fabric:
Costume: Woolen tabby or woolen broadcloth.
Apron: Brocade.
Blouse: Linen.
Stockings: Dutch blue or red.

Jewelry:
No special dress-silver has been designed for this costume.

Shoes:
Traditional black shoes with decorative buckles.

Outerwear:
A jacket has been designed for the costume, the original of which is on display at the Museum of Applied Art in Trondheim.

DETAILS

Colors:

Bodice: Golden or black.

Head-dress: Golden or black.

Skirt, purse and shawl: Black.

Stockings: Black.

Fabric:

Apron: Thin wool, with lining. Floral embroidery; buttoned to the skirt.

Purse: Woolen tabby. Embroidered, and attached at right side of skirt.

Head-dress: Thin woolen hat.

Bodice: Brocade or woolen tabby; side seams; seams on the back as well as the front. The front is fastened by three silver clasps.

Shawl: Thin wool; reversible, one side is embroidered.

Blouse: Linen. Crocheted collar and cuffs; plain shoulder yoke.

Skirt: Woolen tabby. Front plain un-pleated; softly pleated over the hips and shirred at the back. The skirt's bottom edge is reinforced with a red finger-crocheted woven band.

Shoes: Traditional black shoes with decorative buckles.

Jewelry: Special dress-silver has been designed, based on jewelry from the Bronze Age which is on display at the Tromsø Museum.

Ofoten

Designing a costume from Ofoten began in 1975. Gudrun Dalberg, principal of the Narvik School of Arts and Crafts, borrowed 18th and 19th century garments from the Aas farm in Punsvik to exhibit at the 1975 Winter Festival. The Aas farm had been the childhood home of Petra Øien Mohn, and she knew about these garments. Gudrun Dalberg asked her to oversee work on designing an Ofoten costume. Finding additional source material proved difficult, and Petra Øien Mohn asked for help from the local newspapers. Many readers responded with information about former clothing traditions. This, combined with ancient source material, formed the background for the reconstruction of a costume from Ofoten.

Petra Øien Mohn learned of an old skirt from Melkedalen in Ballangen. It had been worn by Mette Bakken, and was about 300 yearsold. Sara Løsett had saved an old golden brocade vest that had been sewn for Mrs. Krogh in Hamnes. The vest had seen better days, but its style could be copied. Legends from the Ofoten area recall the use of black vests as well.

During the war, Petra Øien Mohn found a bridal blouse from 1775 in a chest of old clothes at the Aas farm. She copied the pattern of the blouse, but not its crocheted collar and cuffs. When the Aas farm estate was being settled in 1981, Mohn came across a box of books, and in a book of sermons, she found the crocheting pattern for the blouse from 1775.

Although it was known that the old Ofoten costume had a special apron for church use, none could be found. Great was the joy when Edith Skarstad saw one in the home of a family in Canada. The family had Norwegian forefathers, and the apron was in a frame, hanging on the wall. It had belonged to a girl in Herjangen, Laura Gulliksdatter. The apron was embroidered along the hem, but local flowers were added: lady's mantle, chickweed wintergreen, and barley — in commemoration of the fields that had given sustenance to the people of Ofoten for hundreds of years.

It is cold in Ofoten, and the costume has a reversible shawl with an embroidered side for festive occasions, and a black side for mourning. In the old costumes, pockets were hidden in folds in the skirt. A similar pocket was now visibly mounted on the right side of the skirt. The model for the head-dress is an old garment called "hallekken." This was owned by Ingeborg Harr Hansen, born at Bjellgam in Liland in 1840.

Trøndelag

Efforts to design a folk costume from Trøndelag began in 1920, when three teachers, Ragna Rytter, Kaspara Kyllingstad and Ingeborg Krokstad, recognized the need for a costume for the counties of North and South Trøndelag. They engaged the help of their students in their search for old garments and documentation.

As was often the case at that time, one of the objectives was to use Norwegian fabric, even though they realized that imported fabrics had been used in the past. Previously, linen was cultivated in Norway, and this group wanted to revive old techniques for weaving drill and damask.

The bodice on the first costumes was a drill pattern, with a mercerized cotton warp and a wool weft. Today both the bodice and apron are sewn in damask. Since this costume was being designed for a large geographic area, some optional colors were selected. Based on source material, it was decided that the bodice and skirt could be red, blue, or green. The same damask apron was used for all of these colors.

Numerous shirts were uncovered, and many of these had geometric whitework designs. A number of traced embroidery patterns were also found. Being easier to sew, traced embroidery became the final choice.

There was also a choice of head-dress: either a head-square or a hat with rose-patterned embroidery. The group found many embroidered velvet hats, but to have a lighter hat, it designed one in silk. The linen head-square was a copy of a bridal garment from Selbu. It covered the bride's head on her journey to the church; then she retired to the rectory to dress in her bridal garments. Later, the bride's children were wrapped in this for the christening ceremony. A number of purses with rose-patterned embroidery were found and copied. They are lined in linen, with a leather back section.

The red costume is edged in green; the green and blue are edged in red. The elongated flaps on the bodice and the hemline of the skirt, are also edged.

DETAILS

Colors: Red, green or blue.

Fabric:
Bodice: Damask, woven in linen and wool.
Skirt: Woolen tabby.
Hat: Silk or velvet.

Head-square and blouse: Linen.

Head-dress: Hat with rose-patterned embroidery, or a drawnwork head-square worn over a thick wreath of red wool.

Bodice: Wool edging along the flaps; fastened with two silver clasps at the waist. Double seam stitched at the back.

Purse: Black wool with wool embroidery; leather back piece; special clasp in silver or brass.

Shoes: Traditional black shoes with decorative buckles.

Blouse: Linen with traced whitework on the collar, wrist bands, and chest; plain neckline, and shoulder gussets.

Skirt: Softly pleated; edged in wool, and reinforced with burlap. A linen cord is inserted in the hem.

Stockings: Green stockings are worn with the red costume; red stockings are worn with the blue or green costume.

Jewelry: Special dress-silver has been designed for this costume.

Outerwear: Cape in wool damask; lined in red.

Nordmøre

WOMAN'S COSTUME

By 1920, work on a costume from Nordmøre was already in progress. Karoline Grude at Heimen developed the first one, but it was not considered truly representative of the region.

The Nordmøre Home Crafts Association and the Society of Rural Women continued their work and a new costume was presented in 1939. Unfortunately this costume was lost in a fire during the war. Work on designing a Nordmøre costume continued after the war, and in 1949, a new one was completed. In 1951, the Folk Costume Committee established the final version of the Nordmøre costume.

When the Nordmøre Home Crafts Association started designing outerwear for the costume in 1976, it became clear that the 1951 costume had changed over the years. A committee was formed to work further on the woman's costume. This resulted in a Nordmøre costume that reflects the costume traditions of inner Nordmøre from the early 1800s.

MAN'S COSTUME

This costume was designed by Anna Johannessen in 1922. The magazine "Fra bygd og by" writes that it was based on old pictures and discussions with people in Nordmøre, but this has not been substantiated.

A few years ago, a committee developed a new costume, a reconstruction of one worn in this area in about 1800.

D E T A I L S

WOMAN'S COSTUME

Colors: Black or blue.

Fabric: Woolen tabby. Wool damask.

Apron: Two versions. Checked in cotton and mohair, or white linen with double cutwork.

Head-dress: Linen hat with silk scarf, or tall, pointed hat in black velvet.

Bodice: Four versions: Bright red or dark pink wool damask with bird motifs; blue or green wool damask; pink glossy wool of satin weave with designs (calamanco). The apron is lined in a cotton and linen blend.

Purse: Two versions in red wadmal.

Blouse: Embroidery on collar, wrist cuffs and shoulders. Two variations: Counted threadwork, white on white linen; traced whitework on white linen or cotton.

Shoes: Traditional black shoes with decorative buckles.

Skirt: Coarse woven wool, black or blue. Tightly shirred at the waist.

Stockings: Black or red.

Jewelry: A good deal of dress-silver has been copied for this costume.

Outerwear: Jacket or cape, both in wadmal.

D E T A I L S

MAN'S COSTUME

Colors: Brown knee-britches and jacket. Blue vest.

Fabric: Woolen broadcloth; woolen tabby.

Trousers: Knee-britches with appliqué on front flap and knees.

Garter bands: Multi-colored braided bands.

Jacket: Red appliqué. Three-quarter length, tailored. Worn unbuttoned; row of buttons on either side of front; red buttonholes.

Silk scarf: Can be worn at the neck.

Shirt: Linen; whitework on collar and cuffs.

Shoes: Black buckled shoes.

Jewelry: No specific dress-silver.

Vest: Single-breasted, edged in black; wool embroidery on front.

Rønsdal

Colors:
Skirt: Blue.
Bodice: Red or blue.

Fabric: Woolen broadcloth or woolen tabby. Linen blouse.

Bodice: The elongated bodice has wool embroidery on the front and back; fastened at the front with concealed hooks.

Purse: Same color as the skirt; embroidered; brass clasp.

Head-gear: Hat in same color as the bodice; embroidered at the back; lace edging on the front.

Blouse: Embroidered with counted threadwork, on the yoke, collar and wrist bands, and often on the front opening as well.
For a better fit, most of the blouses have a triangular gusset at either side of the neck.

Shoes: Traditional black shoes with decorative buckles.

Skirt: Border of wool embroidery at the hem; reinforced edge in red, softly pleated except for a flat front panel.

Stockings: Red.

Jewelry: Special dress-silver has been designed for this costume.

Outerwear: A cape in the same color as the skirt.

Work on developing a Romsdal costume began in the 1920s. The model being used for the costume was a plain bodiced dress in checked wool which had been common in the Romsdal area. This costume did not meet with approval; the people of Romsdal wanted a more festive costume with embroidery. The project was set aside. Later, during the Second World War, Mali Furnes developed the first Romsdal costume which was shown in 1947. This is called the "Bolsøy costume" after a township in Møre og Romsdal. The bodice is a copy of one from the late 1700s and early 1800s, found at the Romsdal Museum. The costume as a whole is not a copy, although it was based on old costume pieces. The border of the skirt is said to come from an old underskirt from Bolsøy. When Mali Furnes died in 1968, Olga Talleng continued working on her pattern. In a sense, Olga Talleng and Husfliden in Molde worked side by side on Romsdal costumes. Their fabrics and embroidery colors were different, but otherwise, the costumes were very similar.

When Olga Talleng discontinued her work, she turned her pattern over to Heimen in Oslo. In recent years, the Romsdal Museum has reconstructed two new costumes from the area.

Many old blouses from Romsdal have been uncovered. In "Ung i Romsdal" (no. 6, 1934), Laura Tonberg wrote: "We have many blouse patterns to choose from. I have seen at least 20 variations of this, so it is genuine enough. I have found them in Eidsbygda, Måndalen and Vågstranda. The yoke is based on a bridegroom's shirt sewn by Karen Vik in 1856. The pattern on the wrist bands on this shirt was not especially good, so I took one from an old wrist band sewn by Brit Demmedal. One of the outer borders on the wrist band is on the center of the collar. The blouse should be sewn with white linen thread on white linen."

This is the blouse that is most usually worn with the Romsdal costume; it is worn with all of the versions, and there are also others to choose from.

Sunnmøre

In the 1920s, Klara Semb encouraged the people of Sunnmøre to work on developing a regional costume for festive occasions. She was teaching folk dancing in Sunnmøre and noticed that the "national" (Hardanger) costume and the Hulda Garborg (Hallingdal) costume predominated. The Sunnmøre Youth Organization and the Sunnmøre Home Crafts Association formed a folk costume committee. This resulted in the development of many costumes from the district.

Of these, the Ørskog costume might be the most familiar, not least because Crown Princess Märtha was given one by the Sunnmøre Youth Association as a wedding gift. This is also known as the "Märtha costume." A few years ago, Princess Märtha Louise also received one.

There are two variations of the Ørskog costume. One was designed in Sunnmøre, and the other in Oslo by a group of people who came from the Sunnmøre district. Both groups were working on the embroidery on these costumes at about the same time. On the two costumes, the embroidery on the aprons is similar, but differs on the bodices. The "Sunnmøre" version uses the same pattern on the apron and the bodice, while the "Oslo" version has a design of heart-shaped roses on the bodice. This was probably copied from a bodice at the Norwegian Folk Museum.

Many different blouses are worn with this costume. Some have counted thread-work, some have traced patterns. The latter is most often worn today.

Married women wear a white linen head-square with black embroidery, while unmarried women wear a white head-square with colored embroidery. The head-square is held in place by a "wreath" of black silk ribbon. A black silk hat is also worn.

Nordfjord

Colors:
Skirt: Black.
Bodice: Green or black.

Fabric: Woolen tabby, woolen broad-cloth.

Apron: A choice of two wool aprons.

Head-wear: Hat or head-square; black silk hat with silk edging on the front, and a silk bow tied at the neck. A white head-square is also worn.

Bodice: Decorated with heddle-woven bands on the front, neck, arm openings and back piece. Fastened by eyelets and a silver chain.

Purse: Black; embroidered; fastened to the costume by a special hook.

Blouse: White linen; shoulder yokes; shirred at the neck. Embroidery on the collar, wrist bands, and on the banding covering the front opening.

Shoes: Traditional black shoes with decorative buckles.

Skirt: Pressed pleats; heddle-woven band around the hem. A narrow waist-line is sewn to the bodice.

Stockings: Black.

Jewelry: No special dress-silver has been designed for this costume.

Outerwear: A three-quarter length cape.

As in so many other areas, work on a folk costume for Nordfjord began in the 1920s. Mina Rye developed the first costume, which was shown at a trade fair in Sandane in 1927. This costume was worn until 1947, when the Firda Youth Association established a costume committee to register old garments and to revise the 1927 costume. After collecting historic material, they found little reason for any major changes.

The pattern of the pictured bodice is from Ingeborg Heggen from Heggjabygda. Green, red, blue or black bodices have been worn, but today, most wear green or black. The skirt has pressed pleats. Woven bands decorate the bodice and skirt. The hat design comes from Mrs. Roti, from Eid in Nordfjord. Married women wear hats in patterned silk, and unmarried women wear black silk hats.

Blouses have had both whitework and blackwork embroidery. This blouse can have whitework or cross-stitching in black.

Sogn

WOMAN'S COSTUME

By the late 1800s, folk costumes had fallen into disuse. By the beginning of the 1900s a more festive version appeared. Today's woman's costume from Sogn is based on the plainer costume from about 1800, modeled on costumes from Indre and Midtre Sogn. There have been many different skirts, such as black, blue, green, striped or checked, with varying edging colors. The edges could also be appliquéd and stitched in wool. The skirt could be softly pleated or tightly shirred.

The bodice could be a solid color, striped or patterned, with black velvet edgings. It was fastened by a silver chain and eyelets.

Married women wore a special white head-dress, a wide hat made of thin white fabric edged with tightly shirred lace. For festive occasions, a silk head-band was tied above the lace. Married women wore this hat even after they had discontinued wearing the costume. Unmarried women wore heddle-woven braided bands around the head.

Today the skirt is of black wool with an attached appliquéd edging; usually in red or green. The Historical Museum in Bergen has a number of these. The bodice is sewn in brocade. In more recent times, there has been little variation in these costumes, often because the fabric selection has been poor, but also because women in the same family have wanted their costumes to be similar.

The white linen blouses have counted threadwork in white or black, or both. Married women may wear green silk blouses.

MAN'S COSTUME

This costume is based on the design of men's folk costumes between 1800–1850. The white jacket was worn until about 1860. It is unlined, has a wide back, and is edged in black velvet. The red double-breasted vest worn with this jacket is also edged in black velvet, and has a pocket on either front side. Both the jacket and vest have high, standing collars. Knee-britches with a front flap complete the costume.

WOMAN'S COSTUME

Colors: Black skirt with green or red border. Bodice can be different colors. Blouse in white linen/green silk.

Fabric: Woolen tabby; brocade; silk; linen.

Head-dress: Married woman's hat; wreath of woven bands for unmarried women.

Bodice: Edged in black velvet; no seams at the back; fastened by silver chain laced through eyelets.

Blouse: White linen embroidered at collar, wrist bands and along front opening; shirred neck. Green silk blouse; sleeves puffed at shoulders, tapering off by the wrist bands. Detachable embroidered collar and wrist bands.

Shoes: Traditional black shoes with decorative buckles.

Skirt: Tightly shirred or softly pleated. Appliquéd edging and woolen embroidery sewn at hem.

Jewelry: The dress-silver is not gilded. Married women wear a silver belt.

Outerwear: Cape.

MAN'S COSTUME

Colors: White jacket and red vest, both edged in black. Black knee-britches.

Fabric: Wadmal, woolen tabby, woolen broadcloth, and velvet.

Trousers: Narrow front flap. Four buttons and buckle at the knees.

Head-gear: Brimless cloth cap in red wool edged in black velvet, or hat.

Jacket: Unlined jacket, edged in velvet, no buttons.

Silk neckerchief: Multi-colored silk.

Shirt: Shirred at neck; optional embroidery on collar and cuffs.

Shoes: Black shoes with buckles.

Stockings: White.

Jewelry: No special dress-silver has been designed for this costume.

Vest: Double-breasted; edged in velvet; seven sets of buttons. Lined in cambric; backpiece is cotton and linen blend.

Sunnfjørd

MAN'S COSTUME

This folk costume is inspired by old costumes which are now at the Historical Museum in Bergen. Gunvor Tretteberg worked with Heimen to develop this costume in about 1960. Later, the different parts of the costume were adapted to match the original garments.

The jacket is in red wadmal. It is unlined and has no collar. The front is edged in green and has a richly ornamented band which is also edged in green. There are eight pair of buttons on the front. The jacket is worn unbuttoned. It is slightly longer at the back, and there are two gussets on either side.

There are three tucks at each shoulder, and two vents edged in green on either side, decorated with two buttons. The vest is green, edged in black, and has seven pair of buttons. These are only decorative; the vest is closed by an inside panel. The back of the vest, and its lining, are in a blend of cotton and linen. It has a standing collar and two front pockets. The knee-britches are in black wadmal, and there are four buttons on the front flap.

A linen shirt, modeled on one from the museum in Førde, with drawn work on the collar and cuffs, is worn with this costume.

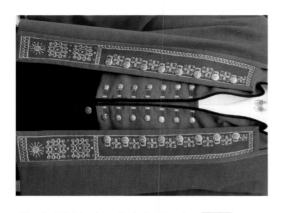

WOMAN'S COSTUME

This costume has been developed by Heimen on the basis of a pattern borrowed from Aslaug Nedrebø in Ålhus. The pattern for the hat comes from Herdis Huus Mannsåker. Two different purses can be worn with this costume. The pattern for the blouse is borrowed from Mrs. Solheim in Florø. It is an elegant blouse which is difficult to embroider, with broad borders of drawn work on the front, collar and wrist bands. Another woman's costume has also been developed in Sunnfjord.

Hardanger

WOMAN'S COSTUME

The Hardanger costume is one of our most popular costumes. We have seen it in paintings from the previous century, and later, as the "national costume," one that was worn everywhere in Norway. National romanticism in Norway reached its peak in the late 1800s. The city folk looked at the people of rural Norway and their clothing traditions with nostalgia. National costumes had fallen into disuse in many rural areas, but in Hardanger, the tradition had been kept alive.

The multi-colored national costume with the fitted red bodice, wide black skirt, and puffy blouse sleeves, was in tune with the fashions at that time. Just before the turn of the century, royal visitors to western Norway, Prince Alexander of Denmark, and Princess Maud of England with her company travelled in exotic Norway. Princess Maud was so enchanted with the Hardanger costume that she ordered one for herself. This costume is now at the Museum of Applied Art in Oslo. It is the costume from the Sørfjorden area that we consider the Hardanger costume. The Hardanger costume varies from area to area, especially the bodice.

The bodice is edged with rose-patterned ribbons, many different patterns are being used. Previously, there was far more variation in the choice of fabric, such as velvet, silk damask, or many types of wool. There are many patterns for the blouse, apron, bodice inset, belt, and belt streamers. Museums along the western coast have many examples of these.

A starched and specially folded head-square for married women belongs with this costume. It is a pity that this head-square is difficult to arrange, because it has resulted in both married and unmarried women resorting to wearing a wreath of woven bands.

MAN'S COSTUME

In Hardanger, the man's costume has a black jacket, red vest and either long black trousers or knee-britches. Knee-britches are most common. The jacket can vary in terms of edging, length and cut. The costume pictured here is from Indre Hardanger, made from a pattern used by "tailor Aarseth." The jacket is edged in red and has green lapels. Along the red edges there is piping in green and yellow. The buttonholes are sewn with green and red thread. The standing collar has a thin border of embroidery. The jacket is worn unbuttoned. The vest has green lapels which are edged in velvet. The buttonholes are the same as on the jacket. The front of the vest and the collar have some embroidery in yellow and green. The vest is double-breasted and has a standing collar.

WOMAN'S COSTUME

Colors: Black skirt, red bodice, white apron, white blouse.

Fabric: Woolen tabby, wool damask, woolen broadcloth, wool, cotton or linen.

Belt: Same embroidery technique as bodice insert. Silver belt with streamers for married women.

Bodice inset: Can be embroidered with beads, cross-stitching or straight stitching. Can also be woven.

Apron: Broad panel of Hardanger (openwork) embroidery. A band for tying the apron is run through a casing.

Head-wear: Head-square for married women; wreath for unmarried women.

Bodice: Broad back, high neck. Front piece has a notch, about 2-2.5 cm deep. Edged in floral ribbon; fastened with concealed hooks.

Blouse: Usually shirred at neck; blouses with plain necks also used. Openwork on the collar, wrist bands and bodice inset.

Shoes: Traditional black shoes with decorative buckles.

Skirt: Can be shirred or softly pleated. Black velvet ribbons can be sewn around the bottom.

Stockings: Black.

Jewelry: Collar button, cuff-links and chain should be silver colored. The rest of the dress-silver is gilded.

Outerwear: Black cape lined in red.

Colors: Black, dark blue, and white.

Fabric: Wool. Poplin blouse.

Bodice: Embroidered on the front and back. A silver chain laced through three eyelets on either side of the bodice front fastens the bodice opening.

Purse: The purse is embroidered and has a clasp.

Head-dress: Fully embroidered cap.

Shoes: Traditional black shoes with decorative buckles. White shoes are worn with the white costume.

Skirt: Draped in folds, with embroidery around the hem. Floral embroidery works its way upward on the skirt.

Stockings: Black for the black or blue costume, and white for the white.

Jewelry: Special dress-silver has been designed for this costume.

Outerwear: A shawl the same color as the costume, and with the same embroidery.

Bergen

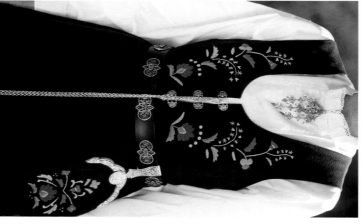

The fashions of the coastal city of Bergen had long been influenced by the larger continental cities in Europe, perhaps mostly those in Germany. In this sense, Bergen has not developed its own special folk costume.

After learning that a folk costume had been developed for Oslo, Bergen also became interested in working on a regional costume. Students at the Bergen College of Art, Craft and Design worked on a design, but their draft was not accepted. A shortage of funds caused their work to be discontinued. Haldis Nygård, who strongly believed that Bergen should have

its own costume, assumed responsibility for designing one.

Haldis Nygård followed the existing guidelines for creating a festive folk costume, and her work was completed in 1956. The costume was to have a fitted, embroidered bodice, a softly pleated skirt decorated with embroidery, and an embroidered cap and purse. The embroidery pattern is based on designs taken from traditional Norwegian floral painting and embroidery. A special blouse, decorated with tatting, is also a part of this costume. Egil Monsen has adapted the dress-silver for this costume from the original jewelry, which was designed in 1870 by Theodor Olsen in Bergen.

Rogaland

WOMAN'S COSTUME

Here too, it was a youth organization that initiated work on a folk costume for Rogaland. The objective was to develop a design for the entire county with an embroidered costume and shawl. Old garments from the area, and the Stavanger Museum served as models. There were many older hat models to choose from in Rogaland, but no embroidered apron was found. Therefore, the embroidery on the shawl and hat were also used on the apron and purse.

The color of the silk brocade bodice is optional. As in the rest of Norway, for some years the lack of fabric variation led to a lack of variation in the bodice.

No complete blouse was found, but some embroidered wrist bands were uncovered, and from these, a design from the first half of the 1800s was chosen. Today the embroidery is either sewn in traced or counted threadwork.

Previously, a tulle head-scarf was often worn on top of the hat, with a bow at the nape of the neck. When tulle became difficult to locate, this custom was discontinued. Today, the scarf is back in use.

DETAILS

WOMAN'S COSTUME

Colors: Skirt: Black, blue or green.
Bodice: Optional color.
Shawl, apron, hat and purse in black.

Fabric:
Skirt: Woolen tabby, wool damask.
Bodice: Silk brocade.
Shawl, apron, hat and purse in thinner wool.

Belt: Velvet belt with silver fastening, or a silver belt.

Apron: Embroidered in wool, attached to waistband.

Bodice: Edged with black velvet and silver ribbons; ribbons also decorate the back piece. Fastened by a silver chain drawn through eyelets.

Purse: Embroidered in wool; hooked to the belt by its clasp.

Head-dress: Fully embroidered hat; scarf covering; white bow at nape of neck.

Shawl: Woolen embroidery; fringed.

Blouse: Embroidered collar, wrist bands and front piece; plain neckline; yoke.

Skirt: Loosely pleated; attached to bodice.

Shoes: Traditional black shoes with decorative buckles.

Stockings: Black or red.

Jewelry: Special dress-silver has been designed for this costume.

Outerwear: A short cape in the same color as the skirt.

MAN'S COSTUME

Work on developing a man's costume ran parallel to the work on a costume for women. Copies were made of garments from the first half of the 1800s, even though these had not necessarily been worn together as a folk costume. The Rogaland Youth Association worked with L.A. Strømme, a tailor.

DETAILS

MAN'S COSTUME

Colors: Black jacket and trousers. Vest in optional colors.

Fabric: Wadmal, woolen broadcloth, silk brocade. Cotton or linen shirt.

Trousers: Long trousers or knee-britches with front flap; edged in red.

Garter bands: Multi-colored finger-braided bands.

Head-gear: Hat.

Shirt: Embroidered shirt or plain cotton shirt; silk scarf in neck.

Shoes: Black buckled shoes.

Stockings: White, green, or two colors red edging. Five pair of buttons on the front; uncut buttonholes. Lapels in same fabric as vest

Jacket: Short with standing collar and red edging. Five pair of buttons on the front; uncut buttonholes. Lapels in same fabric as vest

Vest: Silk brocade or green woolen broadcloth. Double-breasted; with flat lapels and a standing collar. Six pair of buttons.

Setesdal

WOMAN'S COSTUME

Setesdal is one of the few places in Norway where the folk costume tradition has been in continuous use. Many people still live in Setesdal who wore their costumes every day when they were young.

It is often said that the women in Setesdal wear six skirts at the same time. They do not wear six, but they do wear two. The white inside skirt is cotton cambric for the shirt. It is made of wadmal and has a black band at the hem. Above this there are two rows of black woollen broadcloth. A black skirt is worn on top of the white skirt. This has a band of woollen broadcloth in red at the hem, and above this are two rows of wool, one in red and one in green. The band at the hem is reinforced. The red edge on the black skirt should reach to the upper black edge of the white skirt.

The blouse is of cotton cambric, and the collar and wrist bands are trimmed with lace, crocheted lace, or tatting. A short black jacket decorated with green edging, silver ribbons and embroidery is part of this costume.

MAN'S COSTUME

Most people associate long trousers with leather patches on the seat with the man's costume from Setesdal. The costume of today has been in use since the latter half of the 1800s. The trousers have a front bib on the chest-high waistline. They are worn with leather suspenders. The bib is green in woollen broadcloth, edged with leather and decorated with embroidery. A strip of leather runs from the seat patch into the bib. The trouser legs are edged in leather, and have a green embroidered ankle placket with four buttons.

The shirt is in cotton cambric and decorated with lace on the collar and cuffs. A short vest, embroidered on the front, is worn on top of the shirt. The well-known knitted Setesdal cardigan can be worn as well.

WOMAN'S COSTUME

Colors: White under-skirt, black over-skirt. Black jacket edged in green.

Fabric: Wadmal, woollen broadcloth, cotton cambric for the shirt.

Belt: Leather belt with buckle, or a woven band circling the waist twice. The ends of the band should hang at the side or at the back.

Head-dress: Scarf, printed rose patterns on black background.

Bodice: Embroidered back piece and braces.

Blouse: Decorated with lace on the collar and wrist cuffs. The wrist cuffs should show below the sleeves of the jacket. The collar lies over the outside of the jacket.

Shoes: Traditional black shoes with decorative buckles. Setesdal also has special shoes for this costume.

Skirt: The white skirt is shirred to a band and attached to a back piece, which can be embroidered. The black skirt is pleated at the back, and the front is in woollen broadcloth. Otherwise, like the white skirt.

Stockings: Black stockings fastened with woven garters without tassles, or leather straps with buckles.

Jewelry: Setesdal silversmiths have preserved the traditional dress-silver designs.

Outerwear: Black jacket. A shawl is worn over the jacket.

MAN'S COSTUME

Colors: Black, green edging.

Fabric: Wadmal, woollen broadcloth; cambric shirt.

Trousers: Black. The front bib has four pair of buttons. Green piping along the front of the trouser legs.

Headgear: Hat.

Jacket: A short jacket with embroidery and silver buttons is worn in some sections of Setesdal. In other areas a woven cardigan is worn tucked into the trousers.

Shirt: Decorated with lace on the collar and cuffs.

Shoes: Traditional black buckled shoes.

Vest: Short vest with embroidery and four pair of silver buttons. Fastened with a silver clasp.

Aust-Telemark

DETAILS

Optional colors: Black, blue or green. Colored woolen edging.

Fabric: Woolen tabby or woolen broadcloth. Linen or cotton blouse.

Apron: Edged with colored wool; a broad section of embroidery at the hem.

Head-dress: Wreath of woolen bands, or a head-square.

Bodice: Multi-colored woolen embroidery; edged with bands of colored wool.

Purse: Same color as skirt; decorated with the embroidered rose design from the apron.

Blouse: White linen or cotton; multi-colored embroidery.

Shoes: Traditional black shoes with decorative buckles.

Skirt: Shirred at the waist. Broad band of embroidery at the base of the skirt, in the same colors as the bodice; edged in contrasting color along the hem.

Stockings: Black.

Jewelry: Telemark silversmiths have preserved the traditional dress-silver designs.

Outerwear: Red jacket with embroidery on the front; edged with a band of green and yellow.

WOMAN'S COSTUME

This entire outfit is often referred to as the "raud-trøyeklede" from Aust-Telemark. The name stems from its characteristic red jacket, although it could also be green or blue.

The costume was worn until about 1850. It had a short bodice and was decorated with a chain-stitch design on the back. A card-woven belt was tied around the waist. This was a practical element; if necessary, pregnant women could simply loosen their belts. As a rule, the skirt was black, but green and blue skirts were also worn. Borders in various colors around the hem decorated the skirt. The blouse was decorated with multi-colored embroidery, and was often an artwork in itself.

The costume pictured here was developed in 1941 by Heimen. The bodice is based on Plate No. 4111 in *Sømkunst i Norske bygder* (Handcrafts in Rural Norway) by Johanne Bugge Berg. The apron from about 1850 comes from Bø. Mrs. Wergeland loaned it to Heimen, and Mrs. Gulla from Jar copied the pattern for Heimen. The wide section of embroidery at the hem is copied from the apron, and the same colors are used for the embroidery on the bodice. Satin stitching decorates the collar, wrist bands and front of the blouse.

Aust-Telemark

Optional colors:
Jacket: White or green.
Vest: Usually black.
Trousers: Black.

Fabric: Wadmal, woolen broadcloth.
Shirt in linen or cotton.

Trousers: Knee-britches or long trousers; optional green or red piping.

Head-gear: A knitted cap, or a hat.

Garter bands: Multi-colored, hand-braided; woven bands have also been used.

Jacket: Decorated with cutouts in woolen broadcloth. Buttonholes only for decoration. Gussets at the back on each side of the rounded section, emphasizing the unusual shape. The sleeves have only one seam.

Silk scarf: Multi-colored silk scarf; black has also been used.

Shoes: Traditional black shoes with buckles.

Stockings: White or in two colors.

Jewelry: Dress-silver from Telemark.

Vest: Woolen broadcloth, lined in cambric; usually double-breasted, but single-breasted vests are also worn; high, standing collar.

Trousers: Front flap; either knee-britches or long trousers.

Shirt: Usually embroidered in color or in whitework; usually cotton; linen shirts are also worn.

MAN'S COSTUME

This has been in use in Aust-Telemark since about 1830–1840. It has developed from the gray jacket which was widely used in all areas of Telemark. We can assume that this costume, so charactristic of its region, was shaped by creative and skilled tailors. At first, cutouts in black woolen broadcloth decorated the collar, pocket flaps and cuffs. Ola Kolbjørnsrud (1834–1923), a tailor, decorated the front and the semi-circular section on the back. He

may have also been the first to make the jacket in green fabric. At first, knee-britches were worn with this jacket, but gradually, long trousers also came into use. It was the younger men who took to the longer trousers, while the older ones preferred the knee-britches. As the jacket became shorter, the cut of the trousers became higher, and suspenders were added to keep them in place.

Silver buttons were the main decoration on this costume, and there was no lack of them. Often there were 16 silver buttons on the vest, 20 on the jacket, and 27 on the knee-britches.

The jacket has a high, standing collar and flat lapels. The pockets are false. The buttonholes on the front are purely decorative, and are not cut open. Usually there are no straight side-seams, but curved gussets are sewn in to allow for width. Gussets are also at the back of the jacket to give it its special rounded shape.

"Beltestakk" from Telemark

Color: Black.

Fabric:
Costume: Wool.
Apron: Lasting - a sturdy cotton, or wool damask.
Blouse: Linen or cotton.

Belt: Broad card-woven belt.

Apron: Usually sewn in lasting. Wool and silk are also used. Decorated with embroidery; rose-patterned ribbons, decorative borders and lace of gold or silver thread.

Bodice: Can be in a color contrasting to the skirt; decorated with embroidery or ribbons.

Silk scarf: Worn at the neck; can also be draped from the belt as additional decoration.

Head-dress: Card-woven woolen bands encircling the head. Head-square in silk or wool.

Blouse: Many different blouse styles. Collar, wrist bands and front should all be embroidered.

Shoes: Traditional black shoes with decorative buckles.

Skirt: Shirred at the waist; velvet, silk, or woolen damask can cover the reinforced section at the hem.

Stockings: Black.

Jewelry: Telemark silversmiths have preserved the traditional dress-silver designs.

Outerwear: Short, black jacket.

"SASH COSTUME" FROM TELEMARK

As pietism spread throughout Norway, colorful folk costumes were not seen to reflect the ideals and solemnity of the times. Therefore, from 1850 onward, the sash costume came into use. The jacket became black, and all of the colorful borders were omitted. The skirt became very full and was given a broad, stiffened hem. It was said that the skirt should be wide enough to cover the floor of a living-room. The apron was decorated with embroidery and a border of soft earthy colors. Machine-woven fabric was readily available, and was therefore worn more often than homespun.

No new blouse was designed for this costume, but a lowered neckline called for a silk scarf. Some wore two blouses. The card-woven belt doubled in width, and rather than knotting it and letting the fringed ends hang,

they were now tucked into the belt at the waist. A wreath of long woolen bands was still worn on the head, and some women wore no head-square at all, unless they were going to church.

The sash costume from Telemark has been especially popular in the past decade, possibly because the individual can make a personal selection of colors. The danger of this is that the fashions of our time are inclined to call for matching colors, which often result in a pretty, but unimaginative, product.

Vest-Telemark

WOMAN'S COSTUME

The woman's costume shown here is from about 1850. Until about 1820, skirts were pleated and bodices were shorter, and card or heddle-woven bands were wrapped around the waist. The pleated skirts were replaced by the today's shirred skirts. The bodice also became longer. In the 1830s, most waistlines were just above the waist. Skirts could have an embroidered border with an thin edging around the hem. Rose-patterned ribbons were also used.

An embroidered apron had already been part of the pleated skirt costume; and by 1850 the apron borders had become true works of art. The embroidery yarn on these, a rough, carded camel's hair wool, was imported. The festive costume pictured here was developed by Eldrid Robberstad and completed in 1955.

The embroidery pattern on the apron is copied from the Øverland apron from 1830–1840, at Seljord. The embroidery on the bodice is copied from this apron. As far as possible, the embroidery colors are the same that were used in Telemark in the mid-1850s.

MAN'S COSTUME

This was worn in the first half of the 1800s; it has been reconstructed by Eldrid Robberstad. The flap-front trousers were sewn in handwoven wadmal and decorated at the side seams, front flap and knees with thin red piping. This design replaced the pleated trousers that had been in use and required such a large amount of fabric. The hip-length jacket is of natural-colored wadmal. The jacket is tailored at the back, and has two gussets; it has a standing collar with red piping. The front is edged in green, with red piping.

The blue vest in woolen tabby has a standing collar and red lapels. It is single-breasted and has woolen embroidery on the front and the lapels. The handwoven shirt with whitework is made of homespun linen. It has a shirred neck and shoulder gussets, and fine cutwork on the collar and cuffs. Counted threadwork has also been used.

D E T A I L S

WOMAN'S COSTUME

Colors: Black or dark blue with red borders and thin green edging.

Fabric: Woolen tabby; Linen blouse.

Apron: Border of embroidery at hem; trimmed in red, thin green edging. A woven band is attached to the top of the apron so it can be tied around the waist.

Head-dress: Head-squares, one for married and one for unmarried women.

Bodice: Embroidered on front and back; trimmed with red wool; thin green edging. Fastened by a silver chain and eyelets.

Blouse: White linen blouse; shirred neck; embroidered collar and wrist bands, either whitework or a traced pattern.

Shoes: Traditional black shoes with decorative buckles.

Skirt: Shirred with attached embroidered band along the hem; thin green edging.

Stockings: Black.

Jewelry: Traditional dress-silver from Telemark.

Purse: Embroidered in the same color as the costume.

D E T A I L S

MAN'S COSTUME

Colors: White jacket, blue vest, black trousers.

Fabric: Wadmal. Vest in woolen tabby; linen shirt.

Garter bands: Multi-colored bands.

Head-gear: White, brimless cloth cap with red edging.

Jacket: Unlined, with a standing collar; green edging on the front, and thin red piping around the collar, front and shoulders.

Shoes: Black shoes with buckles.

Stockings: White or in two colors.

Jewelry: Dress-silver from Telemark.

Vest: Single-breasted vest with embroidery on the front; front lining in cotton and linen. The back piece is cambric.

Vest-Telemark

Colors: Dark blue, black.

Fabric: Woolen tabby. Linen blouse.

Apron: Rosework embroidery at the hem; narrow woven band sewn to waistband for apron ties.

Bodice: Rosework with herringbone stitching on the front and back; trimmed with bands of red and thin green edging. Three or four eyelets, laced with a silver chain. The eyelets are sewn directly on the bodice, or on red piping which is sewn to the inside of the bodice.

Purse: Same color as the skirt; embroidered with center rose from the apron.

Head-wear: Linen head-square with embroidery.

Shoes: Traditional black shoes with buckles.

Skirt: Shirred, thin waistband; embroidered red band and thin green edging around the hem.

Stockings: Black.

Jewelry: Telemark silversmiths have preserved the traditional dress-silver designs.

Outerwear: A red jacket or a black cape.

Eldrid Robberstad developed three different costumes for women in the 1950s. After a great deal of hard work, she found the original fabric and embroidery colors after searching for documentation both in Norwegian museums and at the Nordiska Museet in Stockholm. Her costumes are based on examples dating from about 1850. At that time the bodices had become longer, which allowed for more rose-patterned embroidery on the front and back.

Historically, there has always been a brass-clasped purse. This fell into disuse because there was no belt to hang it from. When a belt was designed for the costume, with large filigreed buckles, the purse returned. Thinner bands were also used, wound twice around the waist.

A head-square was worn by all married women. This was fastened to a semi-circular piece of padded leather. The everyday head-square was not decorated, but those for festive occasions were works of art in double cutwork on homespun linen and bordered in lace. Head-squares decorated with rosework were also worn.

Unmarried women usually braided woven bands into their hair, pinning the braids around their heads. When they went to church, they wore a head-square placed on a round leather support. At the front of this head-square they wore a strip of red fabric sewn with silver ornaments. The pattern of the apron for this costume is from the Øverland apron in Seljord which dates back to 1830-1840. The rosework on the bodice and the purse is also copied from this apron. Many different embroidery styles are combined on the blouse: Cutwork, a traced pattern, and counted threadwork.

Sigdal – Eggedal

Colors: Black or dark blue skirt and apron.

Fabric: Woolen tabby for the apron and skirt. Silk brocade, wool damask or wool for the bodice. Linen blouse.

Apron: Embroidered; the same length as the skirt. Fastened to the waistline with hooks.

Purse: Same color as the skirt; embroidered and edged in red; hangs from the waist by its clasp.

Head-dress: Fully embroidered, same color as the skirt; edged in red.

Blouse: Shirred neck and embroidered on the collar and wrist bands.

Shoes: Traditional black shoes with decorative buckles.

Skirt: Flat section in front, otherwise shirred; narrow waistband. A broad embroidered border; edged in red. The skirt is held in place by suspenders.

Stockings: Black.

Jewelry: Copies have been made of old dress-silver from Sigdal–Eggedal.

Outerwear: Cape or jacket. Jacket of woolen broadcloth; embroidered edges. Fringed black wool shawl.

In 1938–1939, Heimen, the Sigdal Association of Rural Women, and Carsten Lien, head of the National College of Art, Crafts and Design, went to work on a costume from Sigdal–Eggedal.

They copied the border of a skirt from Øvre Båsum. This border had one red color in the embroidery, but Carsten Lien decided to use four shades of red. Today, this is called the Carsten Lien border. The border with only one red color is also in use, and is referred to as the Båsum border. Two other borders are also worn, one from Hoffart, and one from the Hemstad farm. A bodice that ends just above the waistline is used with all of these skirts. An embroidered apron is part of all of these costumes.

A silk brocade bodice is usually used with the costume embroidered with the Carsten Lien border, but wool damask may also be used. An inset with beaded embroidery is attached in the front opening of the bodice. The costume may also be worn without this piece. Many different blouses are worn, both with white and colored embroidery.

Colored cross-stitching is used, as well as patterns in straight stitches. A multicolored silk scarf is loosely tied around the neck. Both a cape and a jacket have been designed for the costume. The cape is a copy of one from Sigdal; it is made of wool damask and lined in wool. It has an interlining as well, so it is a warm garment. The same cape is used with all of the costumes.

Hallingdal

DETAILS

Colors:
Jacket: White.
Vest: Red.
Trousers: Black.

Fabric: Wadmal for the jacket, woolen broadcloth for the vest and knee-britches; linen or cotton shirt.

Trousers: Knee-britches with a front flap; woolen embroidery on the front of each leg. Silver buttons and a silver buckle at the knee.

Head-gear: Brimless cloth cap made of six velvet-edged pieces of fabric.

Jacket: Front edges in green woolen broadcloth. The sleeves have black velvet cuffs trimmed in red. High standing collar. Three gussets at back; wool embroidery on front, collar, and shoulder flaps.

Shirt: Embroidered collar and a shirred or plain neckline.

Garter bands: Multicolored finger-braided bands.

Shoes: Traditional black shoes with decorative buckles.

Stockings: White, knitted in a braided or knit and purl pattern.

Jewelry: Reproductions of old dress-silver.

Vest: Edged with black velvet ribbon. Three rows of silver buttons on the front; buttonholes on either side. Pocket flaps also decorated with silver buttons.

MAN'S COSTUME

The men of Hallingdal also have a deeply-rooted tradition of wearing festive apparel. The variations that can be seen in the women's costumes throughout the valley do not apply to the men's costumes. This may be because men travelled more than women, and their costumes were made by the same tailors regardless of which section of the area they lived in.

From the early 1800s, the most common garment was a long, white or gray jacket, knee-britches and a red vest, like the one in Valdres. This style did not change until around 1850.

The costume pictured here is from the earlier period. It may have been made for a bridegroom, since regular costumes were probably not as richly decorated. In our time, this festive costume is worn both in Hallingdal and Valdres, with a few differences in the jacket embroidery.

This costume has been very popular among men who have wanted an embroidered costume.

A black costume, called "kortkledu," is also frequently worn. The jacket is short and has silver buttons. The double-breasted vest is also black. This costume is usually worn with long trousers, although knee-britches are accepted. White, or black and white patterned stockings are worn with these.

Øvre Hallingdal

WOMAN'S COSTUME FROM ÅL

The folk costume tradition is deeply-rooted in this valley in Hallingdal. Not many years ago, one could meet older women from this valley who had never worn other clothing than their "everyday" and "festive" costumes. Of course the costumes have changed over the years, in step with time and fashion. Their development has also been influenced by which materials have been available.

The head-dress was an important feature of the national costume. Like most other areas of Norway, married women and unmarried women wore different head-dresses. Upper Hallingdal had a very special head-dress, making the activity of dressing one that required both time and skill. In the early 20th century, a hat was most often worn, and this may have been due to the influence of Hulda Garborg. However in our time, more and more young people have been turning to the older head-dress traditions and learning how to wear them correctly.

In the old days, embroidery and handwork were skills that most women mastered. Many of the embroidered pieces were free-hand, and this allowed for creativity and variations. Today, most of us require a printed pattern for our embroidery efforts. We have fewer colors and types of yarn to choose from, and hence there is less individuality in newer folk costumes.

When Hulda Garborg became interested in folk costumes at the beginning of this century, the Halling costume was the model for what became the "Hulda Garborg costume." The Society of Rural Women of Ål presented her with a beautiful costume when the Bergen-Oslo railroad was opened. The pattern on the pictured costume is from Dortea Perstølen in Ål. It is decorated with beaded embroidery, a characteristic form of ornamentation in the valley.

This area has many different blouses. The whitework embroidery from Hallingdal is unusual as it is sewn on two layers of fabric — usually cotton. A brochure from upper Hallingdal makes a clear statement about how to iron the blouse: "There should be a sharp crease from the wrist bands right up to the collar. Collars must be particularly crisp and fine."

In recent years, everyday costumes have become more common. The feelings of many of the valley's older inhabitants, who have a traditional understanding of when to wear each costume, are expressed by a disapproving woman from Ål: "It has gone so far and become so dreadful, that they baptize their children and even get married in their everyday costumes!"

DETAILS

Color: Black.

Fabric: Wool, wool damask, woolen broadcloth.

Apron: Usually in wool damask with a wide embroidered border at the hem; edged with velvet on the sides; attached to the bodice by an embroidered band.

Head-dress: Hat with wool embroidery.

Bodice: Embroidered in wool; optional edging in velvet; decorated with beadwork.

Blouse: Usually cotton; shirred neckline; whitework or colored embroidery on the collar and wrist bands.

Shoes: Traditional black shoes with decorative buckles.

Skirt: Tightly shirred and attached to the bodice. The decorative band around the hem can be embroidered on canvas or woolen broadcloth.

Stockings: Black.

Jewelry: Hallingdal's silversmiths have preserved the traditional dress-silver designs.

Outerwear: Short black jacket. Checked or printed wool shawl with fringes.

Nedre Hallingdal

WOMAN'S COSTUME FROM HEMSEDAL

Since the folk costume tradition has been strong in upper as well as lower Hallingdal, it has been possible to work from substantial source material. In recent years, folk costume committees in the many different valleys of this area have found a wealth of material. In the long run, this will lead to less standardization and uniformity. We can already note that those who are interested in the history of folk costumes have brought about a revival of the many variations found in older costumes.

The apron shows the most obvious difference in the costumes from upper and lower Hallingdal. In lower Hallingdal, an apron of fine wool with a printed rose-pattern is used on a background of black. White or other background colors may also be worn. Before this fine wool was available, checked woolen aprons were common. These are being copied and worn today.

The whole region uses the same embroidery pattern, but local designs are enjoying a revival because some people have copied privately owned costumes or those found in museums.

The embroidery on the costume in the picture comes from an old hat found in Hemsedal. The antique skirt is dark blue wool damask. The apron is dark blue wool damask. The apron is fifty years old.

D E T A I L S

Colors: Black or dark blue.

Fabric: Woolen tabby, woolen broadcloth, wool damask. Cotton or linen blouse.

Apron: Shirred at the top and attached to an embroidered waistband.

Bodice: Small bodice, usually edged in wool; decorated with woolen embroidery; Nesbyen's costume has a longer bodice with side seams.

Head-dress: Fully embroidered hat, edged in wool. Silk ribbon ties.

Blouse: Shirred at the neck, with embroidery on the collar and wrist bands.

Shoes: Traditional black shoes with decorative buckles.

Skirt: Shirred with a border of embroidery at the hem; edged in wool.

Stockings: Black.

Jewelry: Copies of traditional dress-silver from the valley.

Outerwear: Woolen shawl, either checked or printed.

The new Valdres costume

WOMAN'S COSTUME

Colors: Black or grayish-blue.

Fabric: Woolen tabby or woolen broadcloth.

Bodice: The bodice has a back center seam, and no side seams. Embroidery on front and in center of back. The top five cm of the bodice are left open, and the rest is fastened by concealed hooks.

Skirt: The skirt is gathered in soft pleats matching those on the front panel. The rest of the skirt is shirred. It has a concealed fold in the back. A border of embroidery decorates the bottom of the skirt, which has a 2 cm edging of green along the hemline.

Head-dress: This copy of an old hat from Ulnest is fully embroidered.

Purse: The purse is edged in green and has the same embroidery as the rest of the costume.

Blouse: The same as the blouses worn with the "old" Valdres costume.

Outerwear: The same jacket that is worn with the "old" Valdres costume.

Stockings: Black.

Jewelry: Same dress-silver as for the "old" Valdres costume.

Shoes: Traditional black shoes with decorative buckles.

WOMAN'S COSTUME

When this new costume was being designed, an embroidered costume for Valdres already existed. Discussions about possible changes on the "old" costume may have stimulated the development of a new one. This costume was designed by Heimen Husflid in collaboration with a committee from Valdres.

The cut is a copy of a costume from Semelenge in Vestre Slidre from the 1840s. The fabric was black and red wool, and the embroidery comes from a hat made by Eli Hagen from Utnes, in 1821. The pattern was adapted from a skirt owned by Eli's mother, Ragnhild Lundheim, born in about 1790 in Berge in Utnes.

MAN'S COSTUME

Colors:
Jacket and knee-britches: Black.
Vest: Multi-colored checks.

Fabric:
Jacket and knee-britches: Wadmal; jacket trimmed in velvet. Vest: Cotton and wool front; linen and cotton back-piece.

Shirt: Linen or cotton.

Jacket: Short jacket trimmed in velvet; high standing collar. Seam at center of the back, and two curved seams on either side. Never worn buttoned.

Trousers: Either knee-britches or long trousers, both with front flap decorated with silver buttons. Knee-britches have silver buttons and buckle at the knees.

Vest: Double-breasted with eight pair of buttons; high standing collar, lined in front; the back piece is unlined.

Shirt: Many different patterns in counted threadwork.

Garter bands: Multicolored braided bands worn with the knee-britches.

Stockings: White or patterned in black and white.

Head-gear: Black hat.

MAN'S COSTUME

A committee worked on designing a man's costume; Heimen Husflid helped sew the first model, which was completed in 1962. The jacket is a copy of an older one dating back to about 1865 from Søre Garlid in Nord-Aurdal. The vest is a copy of one from Semelenge in Vestre Slidre. The knee-britches are copied from a pair in the Fagernes museum that once belonged to Ola Bremo, a zither player from Sør-Aurdal, in about 1880–1890.

The Old Valdres Costume

It was Hulda Garborg who initiated work on the model for the first Valdres folk costume. This was as early as in 1914. With this pioneer work, she set the folk costume tradition in motion, and developed a method for designing costumes that is still being used today. Basing her work on old folk costumes, but simplifying them to suit contemporary demands, her designs were based on practicality and loyalty to the special characteristics of the region. She insisted on Norwegian fabric, preferably handwoven, and the costume was to have embroidery in wool.

Aksel Waldemar and Anna Johannessen designed the embroidery pattern for the Valdres costume. The pattern was based on an old gray-brown velvet hat from about 1730 which they borrowed from the Bagn Collections. Portions of the pattern are taken from an old wool-embroidered neckerchief. The cut

of the bodice is based on dresses from the 1840s and 1850s.

The bodice, apron and hat were all decorated with embroidery. The softly pleated skirt was not embroidered. The purse was designed later. Karoline Grude from Heimen recalls seeing this Valdres costume at a folk costume exhibition in 1925. It was brown and worn with blue stockings. Hulda Garborg suggested changing the colors to black and dark blue. In 1948, the Valdres Cultural Committee decided to revise the costume so that it also could be made without an apron, with embroidery on the skirt.

Many blouses can be worn with the Valdres costume. Most of them are in white counted threadwork, but there are also patterns with multicolored cross-stitching.

In 1954–55, Heimen designed an outer garment based on an old pleated jacket from Kaien.

DETAILS

Colors: Black, dark blue.

Fabric: Woolen broadcloth or woolen tabby.

Bodice: Embroidery on the front and back. The back has no seams. The bodice is fastened by concealed hooks, four from the waist and upwards, and one at the top (bell-shaped opening).

Head-dress: Fashioned after an old hat from Bagn, but in the same fabric as the rest of the costume. Fully embroidered.

Purse: Embroidered; same color as the costume.

Blouse: Shirred neck; white or colored embroidery.

Skirt: Wide folded panel at front, remaining fabric softly pleated, meeting at center of back. Correct length is 15–20 cm from the floor.

Outerwear: Pleated jacket, same color as costume.

Jewelry: In recent years copies have been made of a variety of old dress-silver from Valdres.

Shoes: Traditional black shoes with decorative buckles.

Stockings: Black.

Vest-Oppland

A county organization called "Uppland" established a committee in 1937 to reconstruct a Vest-Oppland costume for women.

While searching for source material, Varda Hovstad, wife of the local folk dance leader, found an embroidered sledge cushion from the Augedal farm in Brandbu. This beautiful pillow may come from another area. It may have been made from leftover materials for a larger piece of handwork, such as a coverlet. The cushion is now on display at the Bagn Collections in Valdres. Halfdan Auneberg, head of the National College of Art, Crafts and Design, recommended basing the costume on this embroidery. Heimen in Oslo was then asked to draft a design for a costume. Ingeborg Stenseth's draft was completed in 1939. Halfdan Auneberg's comments were positive, and the members of the Folk Costume Committee who had been included in the work while it was in process, were also satisfied.

The costume embroidery has the same colors as the pillow. The pillow was made of wadmal, but woolen tabby was used for the costume.

Since no models for a bodice had been found, the bodice cut was based on one from an old picture. The white linen blouse has a shirred neckline and shoulder gussets. The embroidery is copied from an antique shawl that Magnhild Strand borrowed from Hadeland. Similar tambourwork shawls were often worn with costumes from the regions of Hadeland and Romerike. The blouse had been designed for the Hadeland costume in 1926-1927 and, in this sense, is older than the Vest-Oppland costume.

In 1979 a committee was established to design outerwear for the costume. A number of old capes were collected but the committee concluded that these were not originally worn with folk costumes. The woman's cape from Heimen was chosen. This short cape is sewn in the costume fabric, and is lined in red.

In 1980 work began on copying old dress-silver. Head curator of the Norwegian Folk Museum, Aagot Noss, assisted with this project. A ring pin, two silver brooches, and cuff-links came on the market in 1983. The bodice is fastened by a spear-tipped silver chain which is threaded through small silver eyelets.

Gudbrandsdalen

THE FESTIVE COSTUME

In 1912, Anna and Aksel Waldemar Johannessen moved from Gjøvik to Oslo and opened a store for patterns of embroidery called "Heimen." Aksel Waldemar was employed by the Norwegian Theater and thereby came into contact with Hulda and Arne Garborg. The need for folk costumes was apparent both at the theater and in the countryside, where Hulda Garborg held folk dancing courses. It was natural for the Johannessen couple to help with this design work.

In 1922, Aksel Waldemar found a blue embroidered bodice at the Norwegian Folk Museum. Legend has it that this bodice was made for a 17-year-old girl from Lom who was to marry a man who was about sixty. Her family must have been wealthy, because three bodices were sewn for her before the family was satisfied. This bodice is now part of the exhibition "People and dress – tradition and use" at the Norwegian Folk Museum.

It was this bodice that inspired Aksel Waldemar Johannessen when he designed the festive costume for Gudbrandsdalen. When he died, a youth organization in Oslo, Bondeungdomslaget, bought Heimen and the rights to the designs made by Aksel Waldemar and Anna Johannessen.

Aksel Waldemar was also a pictorial artist. For a memorial exhibition at the Blomqvist Gallery in 1992, Heimen Husflid uncovered the first costume he designed. The colors proved very different from the ones that were being used in the 1990s. This costume was copied, and it is pictured here next to a contemporary version of the design. The cut is the same as the "Striped Skirt" from Gudbrandsdalen. The apron is optional, but if one is worn, the rose-patterned embroidery higher up on the skirt is omitted. On the first costumes the front of the bodice was fully embroidered. This was discontinued because the embroidery often interfered with the seams. Before the war, the costume could be made in many different colors; today it is either blue or black. The older, original design is also available today. This model has a green bodice, a blue skirt, and a black embroidered border at the hem, as well as a silk apron. The hat is embroidered black silk. A purse for this costume was never uncovered.

D E T A I L S

Colors: Blue or black.

Fabric: Woolen tabby or woolen broadcloth. Linen blouse.

Apron: Black embroidered silk; or black wool.

Bodice: Embroidered on front and back; curved seams from the arm openings at the back. Fastened in front with concealed hooks from the waist upward. The top should not be closed, not even with dress-silver.

Purse: Embroidered; clasp of silver or brass.

Head-dress: Fully embroidered hat.

Blouse: Embroidered on collar, wrist bands and shoulders; shoulder gussets and standing collar.

Shoes: Traditional black shoes with decorative buckles.

Skirt: Softly pleated; embroidered band at hem. If no apron is worn, floral embroidery on the skirt.

Stockings: Black; also white with the blue costume.

Jewelry: Filigree dress-silver or a heart-shaped pendant brooch with crown, is usually worn.

Outerwear: Jacket in same fabric as the costume.

The Graffer Costume and the Rondastakken

DETAILS

THE GRAFFER COSTUME

The inspiration for the Graffer costume is a blue skirt from the 1700s, found at the Graffer farm in Lom. With this skirt as a model, the costume came into use in the 1930s. Its beautiful embroidery made it very popular, and for a long time, it was worn all over Norway. In the 1930s, it had an embroidered bodice, and could be in black or white; the white version was worn with a white silk blouse.

In 1952, the Graffer family and the Home Crafts Association of Gudbrandsdalen completed their work on the Graffer costume as it is today. The Graffer skirt was copied, and since few embroidered bodices had been uncovered in Gudbrandsdalen, the conclusion was that the skirt's bodice had been brocade. Therefore, it was decided that the new costume was to have either a green or red brocade bodice. A blouse from the Graffer farm has also been copied for this costume.

THE "STRIPED" SKIRT (RONDASTAKKEN)

This is one of our oldest costumes. It has been used from about 1830 until today. "Rond" means striped, and therefore we call it the "striped skirt." Today, it usually has a checked bodice, but a solid color can also be used.

The costume has been made in many different checks and stripes. The skirt has an extra fold of material above its hem, and further up on the skirt, there is a pressed crease. A silk apron with embroidery along its hem is optional.

The blouse is in cotton or linen and finished with a picot or tatted edging on the collar and wrist bands. It is worn with a white, starched kerchief which has been folded twice into a square, and ironed to set the creases. The kerchief should be folded and worn so that two ridges appear at the back. It is tied with a special knot beneath the chin.

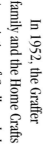

THE GRAFFER COSTUME

Colors: Blue skirt, red or green bodice.

Fabric: Woolen tabby; Brocade.

Bodice: The same cut as the striped skirt costume; fastened with concealed hooks. The top should not be closed, but left open.

Purse: Same material as the skirt; wool embroidery. Attached to the skirt by its clasp.

Head-dress: The wool-embroidered hat is in the same material as the skirt.

Shoes: Traditional black shoes with decorative buckles.

Skirt: Decorated with embroidery; softly pleated and sewn onto the bodice.

Stockings: Black.

Jewelry: Filigree dress-silver is frequently used in Gudbrandsdalen.

Outerwear: Jacket in the same material as the skirt.

THE STRIPED SKIRT COSTUME

Colors: Striped and checked fabric in different colors.

Fabric: Cotton warp, wool weft. Blouse in cotton or linen.

Apron: Woven apron with borders in different colors, or embroidered silk apron, tied in the back with silk ribbons.

Head-dress: Stiffened head-square, or hat.

Bodice: Seam in center of back and curved seams on the sides; checked patterns must meet correctly at the seams. Fastened by concealed hooks from the waist upwards.

Shoes: Traditional black shoes with decorative buckles.

Skirt: Loosely pleated; sewn to the bodice.

Stockings: Black.

Outerwear: Black jacket, preferably in woolen broadcloth.

Colors: Black, dark blue, white.

Fabric: Woolen broadcloth. Cotton blouse.

Bodice: Woolen embroidery on front and back; two curved seams at the back. Fastened with concealed hooks from the waist upward.

Purse: Embroidered; clasp of brass or silver.

Head-dress: The hat has the same embroidery as the costume.

Shoes: Traditional black shoes with decorative buckles.

Skirt: Softly pleated with a band of embroidery toward the base of the hem.

Stockings: Black.

Jewelry: No special dress-silver has been designed for this costume.

Outerwear: A jacket that is identical to the one used in Gudbrandsdalen.

Lundeby

Pictorial artist Ulf Lundeby lived in Lillehammer. He designed a folk costume for a friend, in honor of her 50th birthday, copying the cut of the "Striped Skirt" costume from the valley Gudbrandsdalen. This was in 1932, and embroidered folk costumes were very much in fashion. There were many requests for Lundeby's folk costume. An embroidery shop in Lillehammer, "Søstrene Julin," was given the rights to use his design. Lundeby was born at Tørsæn in Våler, and since he came from this Solør-Odal district, many think that his design can be used as this region's special folk costume.

A plain blouse with a shirred neck is worn with this costume, since no special blouse has been designed.

During World War II, fabric was scarce, and the stores that stocked folk costumes could not supply fabric in the correct colors. Therefore, patterns on the Lundeby costume, and many others, were traced on white or natural wool which was more readily available. This was thought of as a temporary measure, because natural fabric had not previously been used for festive costumes.

Raw silk blouses trimmed in tatting were worn with these white costumes, because it was thought that they were more suitable than the bright white linen blouses.

Nord-Østerdal

WOMAN'S COSTUME

Heimen has been making this costume since the mid-1920s. It has been called the old Østerdal costume, but recently it is referred to as the Nord-Østerdal costume. The design of the bodice is modeled on an older bodice from Trønnes in Storelvdal. Red silk damask is used most frequently, but in the past other colors and fabrics, such as wool damask, were also used. The current scarcity of bodice fabric has led most people to think that the bodice must be red. This is also true of the skirt, which is now usually green or black wool damask. Previously, when it was easier to find many different woolen fabrics, checked or plain material was also used for the skirt.

The costume's blouse is linen with counted threadwork on the shoulders, collar, and wrist bands. It is patterned after two old collarless blouses from Alvdal, which had three-quarter sleeves with cutwork, and an embroidered yoke. Collars had not been necessary then, since it was common practice to wear silk throws around the shoulders. When it became difficult to find silk throws, Kari Kveleng from Alvdal worked out a pattern for a collar and sleeve with wrist bands that was similar to the embroidery on the yoke. In 1936, Heimen made a copy of a purse that had been borrowed from Mrs. Helmer, the wife of a minister in Alvdal.

MAN'S COSTUME

This costume is a copy of one from Østerdalen which is at the Glomdalsmuseet. After consulting with bunad expert Klara Semb in 1961–1962, a few changes were made. This costume has been sewn by many tailors over the years, so the costume details can vary.

DETAILS

WOMAN'S COSTUME

Colors:
Skirt: Often black and green, although other colors can be used.
Bodice: Optional; red is frequent.

Fabric:
Skirt: Wool damask, wool.
Bodice: Silk damask, brocade.

Apron: Handwoven with blend of cotton and wool; checked in red and green.

Bodice: Lined in a blend of cotton and linen. A center seam in the back; side seams are pulled backwards and are double-stitched. Fastened with concealed hooks from the waist upward; single hook at the top.

Purse: Black with woolen embroidery.

Head-dress: Pointed hat. Same fabric as the bodice, or black silk.

Silk scarf: Multicolored silk scarf around the shoulders.

Shoes: Traditional black shoes with decorative buckles.

Apron: Softly pleated backwards from a front center fold; shirred section at the back center; finger-crocheted reinforcement at the hem.

Stockings: Black.

Jewelry: No special dress-silver has been designed for this costume, but dress silver in heart-shaped motifs is worn.

Outerwear: No special outerwear, but a cape is often worn.

DETAILS

MAN'S COSTUME

Colors:
Trousers and jacket: Black.
Vest: Checked, black and red.

Fabric: Wadmal.

Trousers: Knee-britches with a front flap.

Head-gear: "Østerdal Cap," a peaked cloth cap, black.

Jacket: Standing collar with flat lapels; five buttons on either side of front; worn unbuttoned.

Silk scarf: Silk scarf at the neck.

Shirt: Cotton or linen.

Shoes: Traditional black shoes with buckles.

Stockings: White or black rose-pattern on white background.

Vest: Double-breasted, with a narrow standing collar and lapels.

Marie Aaen

In 1941, the board of the Tynset Home Crafts Association set to work on a new women's folk costume for Nord-Østerdal. The existing costumes from this area were not considered festive enough. They had none of the woolen embroidery that was so popular on other regional costumes.

Finding a design that met with everyone's approval was a time-consuming process, and in 1947, Marie Aaen was asked to participate in the board's design competition. Although she came from Tynset, she led the embroidery department at Silkehuset, a fashion house in Oslo. Marie Aaen was famous for her beaded embroidery, and we know that many of Queen Maud's elegant fashions had been created at Silkehuset, possibly through the mastery of Marie Aaen.

By 1948, Marie Aaen had designed a folk costume which would come to be named after her. The shape of the bodice is said to be based on an extended bodice from Storelvdal. The embroidery on the bodice, skirt, head-dress and purse is inspired by decorative floral painting from Olenstua, an old house in Alvdal. The blouse is patterned on the original Østerdal costume, but here, Marie Aaen designed its embroidery, using techniques indigenous to the valley. The jury approved of Marie Aaen's colors and embroidery, but found the costume too heavy and romantic. After further work, in collaboration with Heimen Husflid, the final design was approved in 1948. The costume is either green or black, with black borders on the green, or vice versa. There is also a choice of two head-dress styles, pointed or shirred.

The green costume has a silk apron embroidered with wool. A woolen apron has also been used when silk was difficult to come by. The black costume's hand-woven checked apron is based on one from Fåset in Tynset, now at the Norwegian Folk Museum. Today this costume can be seen throughout Østerdalen, worn by those who prefer richly embroidered folk costumes.

D E T A I L S

Colors: Black with green borders, checked apron. Green with black borders, black silk apron.

Fabric: Woolen tabby or woolen broadcloth.

Bodice: Elongated bodice, edged around the neck and arm openings. The back has one center seam, two curved seams, and side seams. Embroidery in wool around the front, neckline, and following the curved seams on the back. The bell-shaped opening is fastened with two or three pewter clasps from the waist and upwards, and one at the top.

Skirt: Attached to the bodice lining with a front center fold, folds on either side, and a shirred panel in the center of the back. The skirt has an embroidered border above a broad edging of fabric around the hemline.

Head-dress: Two choices: For the black costume, either a shirred hat with a green crown and a black, embroidered brim, or an embroidered pointed black cap. For the green costume, either a pointed black or green hat of wool or black silk, with embroidery.

Purse: The purse is embroidered and has the same color edging as the bodice and skirt.

Apron: Checked apron for the black costume; black silk or black wool with wool embroidery for the green costume.

Blouse: White linen with a traced pattern in whitework.

Outerwear: Long, black cape.

Jewelry: No special dress-silver has been designed for this costume, but a heart-shaped pendant brooch with crown, is usually worn at the neckline.

Stockings: Black.

Shoes: Traditional black shoes with decorative buckles.

Vestfold

Colors:

Skirt: Black or red.

Bodice: Black.

Purse: Black or red.

Apron: White.

Head-dress: Black or red.

Stockings: Black for the black skirt, white for the red skirt.

Fabric:

Skirt: Wool damask. The black skirt is trimmed in green, with a border of silver ribbon. Its bodice is edged in green. The red skirt is trimmed in green, yellow, and has a border of golden ribbon. Its bodice is edged in red.

Bodice: Brocade. The bodice has double seam stitching at the back.

Head-dress: Silk or brocade.

Purse: Wool, woolen embroidery, golden lace.

Apron: Thin cambric.

Shoes: Traditional black shoes with decorative buckles.

Outerwear: No specific outerwear.

Jewelry: Special dress-silver has been designed for this costume. Heirlooms can also be worn.

Efforts to develop a Vestfold costume began early in the 1930s, and the first one was completed in 1932. As in so many other areas, discussions then developed about what a "correct" Vestfold costume should look like. This resulted in a search for additional historical material. As the years passed, a number of versions appeared.

One of the enthusiasts working on the Vestfold costume was Borghild Tranum Røer. After years of research in the National Archives, and old probate records and mortgage registers from Vestfold, Røer confirmed that the folk costumes in Vestfold had never been identical, and had varied greatly in accordance with fashion and availability of fabric. One could refer to a general type, but the details had been in constant fluctuation.

In 1958, Borghild Tranum Røer reconstructed a costume based on ancient garments she had found. The brocade bodice is a copy of a bodice from Veggestad in Vestfold, dating back to the late 18th century. The skirt is reconstructed from descriptions gleaned from written source material. The apron is a copy of one from Andebu from about 1790. There are two purses for this costume. One comes from Tjølling, and the origin of the other is unknown.

As can be seen, this costume is made from elegant fabrics. Vestfold's shipping traditions gave its inhabitants ready access to these popular materials.

As long ago as in the late 1600s, Lorens Berg from Andebu wrote about women's folk costumes in his *History of a Vestfold Community*:

"The woman's costume was more expensive than the man's costume, most often far more expensive. One reason is that women also needed outer garments. A good cape costs about as much as a horse. And they had to have many skirts, which quickly raised the expense."

Østfold

The Østfold Home Crafts Association is responsible for the development of the Østfold costume. A folk costume committee presented the first one in 1936, based on garments and fabrics from the area. The embroidery on the shawl, hat, and purse is patterned after a shawl from the Ellefsrud farm at Idd, near Halden. Two corners of this old shawl were embroidered, one in reds and the other in greens. The green was chosen for one embroidery pattern, while a small "mourning flower," from a shawl found in Askim, was chosen for the other. Shawls often had one side for festive occasions, and the other for mourning. The model for the hat comes from Bossum at Onsøy; for the bodice, from Berg, near Halden; and for the shirt, from a man's shirt owned by Hans Kolberg at Onsøy. Most of the pieces dated back to 1830–1840. The embroidery patterns were traced by artist Elsa Paulsen from Husfliden in Oslo. Klara Semb and Halfdan Arneberg were consultants for the project.

DETAILS

Colors: Black skirt edged in green or red; bodice of green or red, with a pattern of spruce trees; shawl, hat and purse in black.

Fabric:
Skirt and apron: Woolen tabby.
Bodice: Handwoven wool damask.
Shawl and hat: Silk.
Blouse: Linen.

Bodice: Fastened by a silver chain and five pair of eyelets.

Purse: Silk with motifs from the shawl; clasp copied from older model.

Head-dress: The silk hat has motifs from the shawl.

Shawl: Black silk; one corner has a large section of embroidery; the other a smaller one; edged with a small pleat.

Blouse: Embroidered with counted threadwork on the collar, wrist bands and shoulders; shirred neck.

Shoes: Traditional black shoes with decorative buckles.

Skirt: Softly pleated and attached to the bodice; two rows of top stitching above a border along hemline.

Stockings: Black.

Jewelry: Dress-silver has been designed for this costume.

Outerwear: Short, reversible cape; black on one side, and depending upon bodice color, green or red on the other.

D E T A I L S

Colors: Skirt in blue-green wool; bodice in red or golden; skirt in red wool damask; bodice in green or golden.

Fabric: Woolen tabby, wool damask, silk damask.

Bodice: Thinly edged around neck and sleeves with same fabric as skirt. Double seam stitching at the center of the back.

Skirt: Soft folds with embroidery in ivory colored wool yarn and embroidery floss.

Head-dress: Hat trimmed with handmade lace in skirt fabric; same embroidery as border of skirt; thinly edged with bodice fabric.

Purse: Same color, embroidery similar to skirt. Edged with bodice fabric.

Apron: White linen with cutwork.

Blouse: White linen with cutwork.

Stockings: Black for the blue-green skirt; black or white for the red skirt.

Outerwear: Black wool damask cape with red lining.

Jewelry: Special dress-silver has been designed for this costume.

Shoes: Traditional black shoes with decorative buckles.

Følo

Follo's first Folk Costume Committee was established in 1954; later, representatives from the Society of Rural Women in Follo joined the committee.

Originally, the plan had been to create one costume for the whole county of Akershus, but since the township of Romerike already had its own costumes, this idea was put aside.

The committee first decided on a red silk damask bodice and checked wool skirt in turquoise and brown, but response to this was poor, since it had no embroidery. The next design was presented in 1963, after the committee came upon a fragment of a bridal cloak that had been part of a 1953 exhibition of old textiles at the Norwegian Folk Museum. This bridal cloak came from Herrefossen in Rakkestad, and dated back to 1750. Thora Skallerud designed and simplified its embroidery.

This folk costume met with success, and with the help of Husfliden its final design was established in 1970. The skirt fabric can be either a blue-green woolen tabby or red woolen damask. The bodice is of silk damask and is thinly edged with fabric from the skirt. The bluish-green skirt has a red or deep yellow bodice, while the bodice on the red skirt is green or deep yellow. The blouse and apron are embroidered.

Inspiration for this embroidery comes from an ancient sampler from Søndre Gausdal in Såner. The purse's shape and clasp are reproduced from one that belonged to Amalie Goavim (1851–1942), from Kroer.

Handmade lace trims the head-dress which has the same fabric and embroidery that are recommended for the border of the skirt. For outdoor wear, there is a cape in the traditional style of eastern Norway. Special dress-silver has been designed for this costume. The married woman's belt, and the clasp on the cape are both reproductions from older folk costumes.

Rømerike

L 40:

Work was underway on a Rømerike costume as early as in 1920, but the early costumes had no embroidery and were not met with enthusiasm. In 1932, Borghild Tranum Røer found an old purse from Ullensaker, and its embroidery pattern was used for a new Rømerike costume. The first model was presented at the Rømerike Youth Association's annual meeting in 1936. It was red with yellow embroidery on the bodice and apron. Work continued on this model, and in 1940, it was completed. At that time, the apron was optional, and most people omitted it. Borghild Tranum Røer later regretted this option, since she felt that the apron was as much a part of the costume as the hat was. Today, the apron is usually worn.

Fabric and embroidery yarn were scarce during the war, and some Rømerike costumes were sewn in red yarn, while others were made from black fabric. Today the costume is embroidered in two shades of yellow wool, and the French knots and filling stitches are sewn with embroidery floss. The floral pattern on the back is optional, but if it is used, the belt should not have any embroidery.

There are two embroidered linen aprons for this costume, as well as one in natural printed linen with a brown pattern. This apron was often worn in the 1950s, but when the fabric became difficult to acquire, it was forgotten. Today it is back in use.

L 55:

In 1955 a new Rømerike costume was designed. Borghild Tranum Røer had found a shoe from Enebakk or Fet dating back to the 1700s. The shoe was in red wool, with white embroidery. This time, the bodice was brocade, trimmed with velvet and a decorative golden border. The cut is the same as the L 40 costume, but the assembly of the bodice is somewhat different. Two blouses have been designed for the Rømerike costumes. Ingeborg Stenseth made the pattern for one of them, which is inspired by an old throw. This one is decorated with French knots and chain-stitching. The other is embroidered in satin stitching in a pattern based on wood-carving from Ullensaker.

DETAILS

BOTH L 40 AND L 55:

Blouse: Shirred at neck; white embroidery on the collar and wrist bands.

Jewelry: Special silver has been designed for the costumes.

Stockings: White.

Outerwear: A jacket has been designed for the costumes.

Shoes: Traditional black shoes with decorative buckles.

DETAILS

L 40:

Colors: Blue, green, red and blue-green.

Fabric: Woolen tabby, blouse in linen.

Apron: Embroidered wool in the same color as the skirt; white embroidered linen, or printed, natural linen.

Bodice: Embroidered on front and back; fastened at the front with silver hooks, two or three by the waist, and one on the top.

Purse: Same color as the skirt; embroidered. The clasp is a copy from an old purse.

Skirt: Embroidered at the hem; softly pleated with an attached narrow waistband. The skirt is sewn to the bodice.

Head-dress: Same color as the costume; embroidered. Two versions: a pointed hat and a hood.

L 55:

Colors: Red or blue-green.

Fabric: Woolen tabby; Brocade bodice.

Apron: Wool with embroidery; the apron described for L 40 can also be worn.

Bodice: Edged with velvet and golden ribbons; double seam stitch at the back; fastened at front with concealed hooks.

Purse: Same color as the skirt; woolen embroidery.

Head-dress: Same color as the skirt, with woolen embroidery.

Skirt: Embroidered along the hem; softly pleated, waistband attached to bodice.

Romerike

WOMAN'S COSTUME L 46

Work on a second Romerike costume was started in 1937 by Borghild Tranum Røer and Karoline Grunde from the Romerike Youth Association. The starting point was the embroidery on an old saddle blanket from Enebakk. On this costume, the bodice was elongated, based on a jacket worn by Margrete Norum (b.1781) from Sørum. The hat was a copy from Sørum, from about 1770. This costume was completed in 1946, and it was red, green, or blue-green. A two-colored costume was also used, with a red bodice and a blue-green skirt. The hat and purse match the bodice, and the blouse worn with the other Romerike costumes is also worn with this one.

MAN'S COSTUME

This costume was completed in 1952. Åsmund Seimdal from Kolbotn, and Heimen's joint work was based on old costume pieces and a painting by Anders Hanneborg from Høland. The tailored jacket is in white wadmal, and falls 10 cm above the knee. There are five buttons and uncut button-holes on the front. In the old days, one could tell where people came from by the color of the buttonholes. The jacket has no pockets, only pocket flaps. It is lined in red cotton. The vest is a copy of a cotton vest from Elton in Nannestad. Today, the material is woven in a blend of cotton and wool. The vest is single-breasted, with seven buttons; it has front pockets and a standing collar.

The knee-britches have a front flap, a style that was common in about 1750. Their style is not necessarily associated with Romerike. There are five buttons on the front flap, and three buttons and a buckle above each knee. The shirt was designed for this costume on the basis of one from Trøgstad. It is white linen, with embroidery on the collar and cuffs. No special headwear is designed for the costume, but a hat is worn.

WOMAN'S COSTUME L 46

Colors: Red, green, blue-green.

Fabric: Woolen tabby. Linen blouse.

Apron: A printed linen apron can be used.

Bodice: Elongated, woolen embroidery; thin woolen piping. Fastened with three clasps from the waist, and one at the top.

Purse: Embroidered; same color as the bodice.

Head-wear: Embroidered hat; same color as the bodice.

Shoes: Traditional black shoes with decorative buckles.

Skirt: Embroidered border along the hem; edged in wool. Softly pleated, with approx. 10 cm shirred section at the back; skirt is attached to the bodice lining.

Stockings: White.

Jewelry: Special dress-silver has been designed for this costume.

Outerwear: Long cape; black lined in red.

MAN'S COSTUME

Colors: White jacket, blue striped vest, black knee-britches.

Fabrics: Wadmal, cotton and wool blend, linen shirt.

Garter bands: Multicolored hand-braided bands.

Headwear: Hat.

Jacket: Lined in red, standing collar; tailored side seams; false pockets.

Shirt: Shirred neck; embroidery on collar and cuffs.

Shoes: Black buckled shoes.

Stockings: White, with pattern.

Jewelry: Special dress-silver has been designed for this costume.

Vest: Single-breasted, standing collar; back piece and lining in blend of natural cotton and linen.

Oslodrakta

Tracing back to a folk costume originating from the Oslo area started later than in the rural districts. Like other larger Norwegian cities, European influence has been strong, and this has contributed to clothing styles changing more often than in inland Norway.

When it was decided to design a folk costume for Oslo, the idea of what a festive costume should look like was more important than reconstructing a costume based on traditions in the area.

In 1947, Steen & Strøm, a department store in Oslo, decided to design an Oslo costume in connection with celebrating the store's 150th anniversary. Also, Oslo was preparing for its 900-year jubilee in 1950.

The manager of the embroidery department, Harriet Henriksen, composed the costume, and Ingeborg Solum designed the pattern. The embroidery on the bodice, skirt and head-dress depict the midsummer flowers of Oslo's forests, and St. Hallvard, the patron saint of Oslo, is the motif on the purse.

The entire costume is made of wool, with a blue hat, a bodice of light blue, and a light-blue skirt with a broad band of gray wool slightly above the hem. The style of the shirt has changed somewhat over the years, but it has always been pearl gray. Originally the shirt was shaped like a blouse, with a small folded collar, buttons down the front, and long cuff-linked, set-in sleeves gathered at the shoulder.

Recent owners have added new accessories, such as a head-band and a belt with silver ornamentation. One can assume that the intention has been to add the decorative elements that are commonly included in many other folk costumes.

ST. HALLVARD

St. Hallvard (1020–1043) is the patron saint of Oslo. According to legend, he was the son of a chieftain, Vebjørn, from Huseby in Lier, whose wife was St. Olaf's mother's sister's daughter. The legend relates that he was killed by an arrow while in a boat on the Drammensfjord, trying to rescue a pregnant woman from her pursuers. His body was tied to a millstone and thrown into the fjord, but the body and the millstone resurfaced and were found by the local people. This was seen as a sign that he was a saint. St. Hallvard was later enshrined in the Oslo diocese church which was then dedicated to him. He is the main motif on Oslo's coat of arms.

DETAILS

Colors:
Costume: Light blue.
Stockings: White.
Fabric: Woolen broadcloth.

Bodice: Heart-shaped neckline; embroidery on front and back; fastened with one clasp.

Head-dress: Embroidery on crown of hat. Gathered folds at the nape.

Purse: Embroidered, with "Oslo" engraved on its clasp.

Shirt: Pearl grey; blouse-shaped.

Outerwear: Cape in the same fabric as the costume, reaching down to the top of the embroidered panel of gray on the skirt.

Jewelry: Special dress-silver has been designed for this costume.

Shoes: This costume has its own special shoes.

Detail of a bridal costume from Setesdal in the latter half of the 19th century. Borrowed from the Norwegian Folk Museum.

How to care for ana

Store your folk costume

Slangesølje, dress-silver from Bø in Telemark. Borrowed from the Norwegian Folk Museum.

If you are fortunate enough to own a Norwegian folk costume, you certainly want to take good care of it. It has been made from many natural fibers, and these need air. A folk costume must never be stored in a plastic bag! After wear, it should be hung outdoors and given a good airing. Remove any stains and shake it carefully.

If the costume needs to be cleaned, it is wise to take it to an expert dry cleaner. After it has been cleaned and aired, place it carefully on a hanger. Sew generous loops on the inside of the waistband, turn the skirt inside out, and let the bodice hang down into the skirt. The skirt loops can then be attached securely to a hanger. The apron should also hang freely.

After this, find an old cotton sheet and wrap it loosely around the costume. For a more distinctive covering, you could sew a clothing bag with a decorative border and an embroidered date. It is always a pleasure to store your garment this way. It needs to hang freely in the closet; if this is impossible, it is better to hang it in an attic or in another suitable storage place.

Your shoes also need care. Clean and polish them before storing them in a box. Or you might want to sew a bag for them too. Cloth bags for the costume accessories are also practical; they will keep everything in one place. Following this simple advice will guarantee that your costume will always be ready to wear.

It is important to wear your folk costume correctly. This means that all of the pieces that belong to the costume should be worn. If there is a special head-dress, wear it as well. Many find it difficult to keep their head-dresses in place, and this is true when trying to fasten them over newly washed hair. When planning to wear a cap or head-dress, save the expense of a hairdresser and you will have far less trouble. Also, remember that the stockings should be opaque. As an extra precaution, if you

have a purse for your costume, it is wise to fasten it from the inside of the skirt with a safety pin. A folk costume skirt will hang especially well when it is worn over a cotton underskirt. You can make this yourself. You might want to sew an inside pocket on the underskirt.

Wash and care of a folk costume blouse

Sewing and embroidering a cotton or linen blouse takes many hours of work, and it is important that it is treated with care. Sometimes the collar and wrist cuffs are of linen, while the rest of the blouse is cotton. In this case, the blouse must be treated as if it is all linen. Linen blouses must not be washed at more than 60 degrees Celsius (140 F). If the blouse has turned yellow, it might help to warm it up in soapy water. Bleaching on the snow in the Spring is a tried and true method; chlorine bleach is not recommended for cotton or linen. The blouse can well be washed in a machine, but to save wear and tear, it is a good idea to put it in a pillow case. Rinse the blouse very well to avoid staining or discoloration when it is ironed.

After wearing the blouse, it is best to wash it before putting it away. It should not be ironed when it is put away, otherwise it will turn yellowish. Nor should it be placed in a plastic bag. Cotton and linen are natural materials and need air. Wrap the blouse in an old, soft towel, or a pillow case.

Should you want to take a little extra time, you could sew a special bag for the blouse. Decorated with initials and date, it will be a thing of beauty in itself. Wash the material for the bag well, in order to remove the sizing.

Ironing the blouse

Sprinkle the blouse with lukewarm water, pack it tightly in a towel and let it rest overnight in a plastic bag. DO NOT FORGET IT! Set the iron on the wool setting, and start by ironing the blouse inside out. Embroidered sections must be ironed on the reverse side on a soft undercoating. If the collar is a bit tight, it can be stretched a little when it is damp. Turn the shirt right side out and run the iron lightly over it. Let the blouse hang to dry until the next day. Then it can be ironed on the right side. This process takes time, but the blouse will stay smooth longer.

There are different practices about whether a blouse should have a pressed crease on the sleeves; find out how the blouse for your particular costume is usually ironed.

Make your costume blouse a little extra special. Embroider your initials and the date below the front opening, or along the hem. This will make your blouse an even finer family heirloom.

Take good care of your dress-silver

Since folk costumes are not worn very often, dress-silver can easily become tarnished between the times it is used. Certain steps can be taken to avoid this. Silver should always be stored in airtight plastic bags, such as the "zipper" bags. Use a separate one for each piece of jewelry to avoid scratches. Nevertheless, a good cleaning is necessary every once in a while. A mixture of dishwashing detergent and ammonia does wonders; heat the mixture, and add the silver; after a short soak, rinse it well under running water, and dry it carefully with a soft cloth.

If the silver has become extremely tarnished, it is best to ask a jeweller to clean it. Do not fall for the temptation to dip oxi-

Jacket clasp in silver from Telemark. Borrowed from the Norwegian Folk Museum.

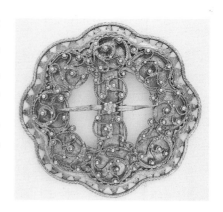

Trandemsølje, dress-silver from Nes in Telemark. Borrowed from the Norwegian Folk Museum.

dized silver into a self-cleaning "silver dip." It will be ruined. A foaming polish is a good solution. If you have silver clasps on your costume, do not try to polish them while they are attached to the material; the entire costume will end up at the cleaners. If the clasps need a good polish, clip them off before polishing them. I have also heard that "dress-silver should be allowed to age with its costume." Maybe this is true; it is a matter of personal preference.

On a man's costume, silver buttons can be polished without removing them by cutting a slit in a piece of cardboard and slipping the slit around the base of the button to cover the surrounding fabric.

I would also like to make a point about having a permanent brooch hole in the shirt. Decide where the hole should be on your shirt after ensuring that the brooch will be securely centered. Push a thin knitting needle through this hole and then whipstitch around its circumference. In this way, you will always know where to place the brooch. Not only will it be easier to pin it on correctly, the blouse will not wear out as quickly.

On most folk costumes, the silver ornaments are worn on the blouse, not on the bodice.

It would be wise to wrap your silver belt in acid-free paper before placing it in its plastic bag. It is always helpful to keep all of the costume's accessories in one place. Wooden boxes can be purchased in different sizes. Find one that is large enough for all of your "bits and pieces" such as the jewelry, purse, silk scarf, stockings etc. If you have a creative flair, you might even want to paint your name and the date on the side or lid of the box.

© Boksenteret A/S, 1996

2nd printing 1996

Desktop-published by Boksenteret A/S

Design: Elin Sollesnes, Boksenteret A/S

Prepress: Tangen Grafiske Senter AS

Print: Tangen Grafiske Senter AS, Drammen 1996

Paper: 150 gr. Galerie Art Silk

Photo: Frits Solvang

Translated by Ann Clay Swick and Brit Henschien

Boksenteret A/S

Postboks 3125 Elisenberg

0207 Oslo

Telephone: (+47) 22 54 07 00

ISBN: 82-7683-088-9

This book has been published in cooperation with
Heimen Husflid, Oslo.